P9-CDA-114

Please Don't Say You Need Me

Biblical Answers for Codependency

JAN SILVIOUS

PYRANEE BOOKS

Zondervan Publishing House
Grand Rapids, Michigan

Please Don't Say You Need Me:
Biblical Answers for Codependency
Copyright © 1989 by Jan Silvious

Pyranee Books are published by the Zondervan Publishing House
1415 Lake Drive, S.E., Grand Rapids, Michigan 49506

Library of Congress Cataloging-in-Publication Data

Silvious, Jan, 1944–
    Please don't say you need me : biblical answers for codependen-
cy /
    by Jan Silvious.
        p.   cm.
    "Pyranee books."
    ISBN 0-310-34391-7
    1. Relationship addiction. 2. Relationship addiction—Religious
    aspects—Catholic Church. I. Title.
RC552.R44S55   1989
158'.2–dc20   89–34337
                                                            CIP

Edited by Linda Vanderzalm and Nia Jones

Printed in the United States of America

89   90   91   92   93   94 / ML / 10   9   8   7   6   5   4   3   2

Dedicated
to
Debra Martin, who faithfully challenged me to soar
even when I had wounded wings

to
Carolyn Capp, who consistently encouraged me to
keep going,
and gently helped me do it

and to
David, Jonathan, and Aaron,
who have given me my life's greatest joy—
being their momma.

Contents

Acknowledgments

This book has been shaped by the influence of some wonderful people God knows I need in my life.

— Kay Arthur taught me to love the Scriptures with my whole heart.
— Marie Chapian taught me to face the unknown with a sense of adventure.
— Lori Rentzel taught me the phrase "emotional dependency" and got the wheels of my mind turning.
— Debra Martin read and commented with her own special brand of encouragement.
— Carolyn Capp typed and retyped with her own special brand of "This is fun!"
— June Hunt prayed with a friend's devotion.
— Suzanne Goebel cheered from afar.
— Betsy Bird is still waiting to see the manuscript—and loves me anyway!
— My sweet husband, Charlie, gave the time and freedom I needed to write for days . . . weeks . . . or was that months, Honey?
— And my mom and dad believed, as usual.

My heart is full of gratitude for each of you.

Definition of Terms

Dear Reader,

As you begin to read *Please Don't Say You Need Me,* I ask you to do two things . . .

(1) Pray that God the Holy Spirit will lead you into truth as you encounter new thoughts and concepts.
(2) Put aside your preconceived ideas about the topic of codependency.

I have read codependency experts from many arenas and have found they share a common bond: the inability to clearly define codependency. According to Anne Corwin, a specialist in the field, "Codependency is not a new disease, but it has only recently been named. This label was applied in 1979."[1] And, according to Melody Beattie, another expert, "Codependency has a fuzzy definition because it is a gray, fuzzy condition. It is complex, theoretical, and difficult to completely define in one or two sentences."[2]

So, in the light of this confusion, I think it is important to establish definitions that will apply to this book alone. I have developed these definitions and am spelling them out at this point so you might have a clear point of reference from the very beginning.

CODEPENDENCY: Throughout the book you will encounter a situation called "codependency." This is a *relationship* between two people who allow one another's behavior to profoundly affect each other. In an attempt to "feel good" about himself, one will try to control the physical, emotional, and spiritual behavior of the other. The other will compromise physical, emotional, and spiritual well-being for the sake of the one.

THE EMOTIONALLY DEPENDENT PERSON: This is the individual in the relationship who is the primary dependent. This person views connection to another person as the essential source for his self-esteem and security. This is the weaker of the two people in the relationship who leans on the stronger, yet controls the stronger with his manipulation and his great neediness.

THE CODEPENDENT PERSON: This is the individual in the relationship who is stronger but easily controlled by the neediness of the weaker, emotionally dependent person. The codependent will compromise his own well-being to meet the needs and to protect the feelings of his leaning, emotionally dependent family member, friend, or co-worker.

For the sake of clarity, I have tried to specify the differences between emotionally dependent and codependent throughout the book. If there is a situation where delineation is not applicable, the words "dependent" or "dependency" will be used.

Comes the Dawn

After a while you learn the subtle difference
　Between holding a hand and chaining a soul,
And you learn that love doesn't mean leaning
　And company doesn't mean security,
And you begin to understand that kisses aren't
　　contracts
　And presents aren't promises,
And you begin to accept your defeats
　With your head held high and your eyes open,
With the grace of a woman, not the grief of a child.
　You learn to build your roads
On today because tomorrow's ground
　Is too uncertain for plans, and futures have
A way of falling down in midflight.
　After a while you learn that even sunshine
Burns if you get too much,
　So you plant your own garden and decorate
Your own soul, instead of waiting
　For someone to bring you flowers.
And you learn that you really can endure,
　That you really are strong
And you really do have worth
　And you learn and learn . . . and you learn
With every goodbye you learn.

—author unknown

1

What's Wrong with Me?

CASE ONE

My telephone rang at 10:00 P.M. The sad voice was too familiar. In half-apologetic, half-desperate tones she said, "You have got to tell me if I'm going crazy."

For nine years, my friend Margaret had called periodically to say her adulterous, abusive husband was once again trying to charm his way into her affections while continuing to live in adultery with his secretary. All it took from him was a kind word or a tender touch, and momentarily, the rage within her was silenced as she hoped against hope that maybe this time they would salvage their marriage.

During their lives together, he had threatened her, lied to her, abandoned her, and been unfaithful to her. Yet whenever I would suggest that we are not intended to live continuously in such relationships, she would whimper, "But, if I don't have him, I'll be all alone. Just having him part of the time is better than not having him at all."

For years her drama has had the same story line. He cheats, she gets angry and threatens to leave. He repents with sweet words and plays the role of devoted husband. She convinces herself he has changed. He cheats, she gets angry, and the cycle starts all over again. Each time, her spirit dies a little more, and yet she can't find a way of escape.

CASE TWO

The attractive businesswoman took me by surprise as she told the bizarre tale of chasing her roommate around the block, begging her to come home after they had quarreled. Lynn poured out her feelings of rage and disappointment about her friend Diane.

Lynn's childlike brown eyes looked pouty as she detailed Diane's inconsiderate actions toward her. This roommate, with whom she had shared everything, was slighting her, spending too much time with another woman at work. Their frequent arguments always seemed to be ignited by the failure of one to meet the other's need for companionship. The weekend had been a repetition of so many others.

Lynn had wanted the two of them to go to a movie, but Diane already had made plans with her friend at work. The nagging and accusations began, and in an outburst of frustration, forty-year-old Diane stormed out of the house, vowing never to return. Lynn ran out after her, begging her to talk. Through tears, Lynn promised that she would be better if Diane would just come home.

CASE THREE

Many years ago I met a wonderful friend. We clicked immediately. We enjoyed doing many of the same things. We loved to talk and dream, and we liked the way our friendship felt. It became a real comfort zone for both of us. Whenever I needed to talk, she was there. Whenever she wanted to go somewhere, I went with her.

The easy camaraderie and the heady feeling of immediately becoming "best friends" flattered our egos. My friend needed me and I loved being needed. Every protective, encouraging thing I did was received as a precious gift. Her gratitude was unending, and I loved it.

Then one day things changed. I can still remember the dark cloud that quietly floated across my comfort zone. Someone else had come on the scene. She was bright, bubbly, and loved to do fun things with my friend. It soon became evident that I was not needed very much anymore.

At first my reaction was one of slight annoyance,

similar to the response you have to the buzzing of a mosquito in your ear. Then my feelings became irritated. The irksome bug had bitten me. As the welt of anger and irritation grew, I realized I had been attacked by jealousy. That made me furious with myself and even more furious with my friend and her friend. Soon the welt was scratched raw and a full-blown infection set in. It didn't take long to spread, and ugly open sores appeared for all to see. The healing of those infected areas took a long time because the jealousy episode was just one of many irrational, destructive scenes to be played out in our relationship.

Today, the sores are healed, but the scars remain as silent reminders of an agonizing time when a relationship controlled my emotions and consumed energy that should have been more profitably given to other relationships and activities.

CODEPENDENCY

While the circumstances differ in each of these cases, the root problem is the same: codependency. This root grabs hold of the soil of your heart so firmly that pulling it up and destroying it is a phenomenal task. It takes time, determination, and an unshakable faith in God and his power to intervene in your life.

What is codependency? Simply put, it is a relationship between two people who allow one another's behavior to profoundly affect the other. In an attempt to "feel good" about himself, a participant in a codependency will try to control the physical, emotional, and spiritual behavior of the other person, or he will compromise his own physical, emotional, and spiritual well-being for the sake of the other person. Both the control and the compromise are predicated on the belief that this relationship must exist for personal esteem, security, and intimacy. This is a very clinical description of a heart-rending, destructive situation that kills many relationships and breaks the spirits of people who had nothing but good intentions when they first met.

Unfortunately, one of the laws of human relationship is if we look to another person for security, intimacy, and esteem and can't receive enough, the relationship will crumble. No one can sustain the unrealistic expectations of another, no matter how dear that person is, if he feels responsible to give the impossible. Eventually the intense demands will crush the relationship's life and spontaneity, leaving only obligation and resentment. And for the individual who feels so desperately needy, disappointment after disappointment will set up a track record for failure in every significant relationship. Misery will only compound as his search for security, intimacy, and esteem goes on.

All of us, whether we choose to admit it or not, have dependency needs and feelings. "But for most of us these desires or feelings do not rule our lives; they are not the predominant theme of our existence. When they do rule our lives and dictate the quality of our existence, then we have something more than just dependency needs or feelings. We are dependent."[1] Despite the needs we all have, we are healthy when we retain the ability to make choices in our relationships. We can choose to stay and work on difficulties. We can choose to leave. The freedom and health is found in the fact that we can choose!

Because every relationship involves two or more people, in every codependent relationship, there is one person who is the primary dependent. This individual views connection to another person as the essential source for self-esteem and security. For the sake of clarity, throughout the book, I will refer to this person as the emotionally dependent or the weaker individual in the relationship. The codependent in the relationship is the individual who is the stronger of the two. This person views caring for the needs and protecting the feelings of the emotionally dependent person as vitally significant for his self-esteem and security.

Ironically, an emotionally dependent person in our

relationship can become the codependent in another relationship. This may seem confusing until you understand that control and compromise can vacillate back and forth depending on the state of the relationship at the moment.

Dependent people often continue to hang on to a relationship even when the other person is unattainable or has made his or her lack of interest clear. Codependent people often stay in situations where they have nothing in common, where they have ceased to enjoy the other person, or where they are desperately lonely or emotionally assaulted. And although it takes two to make and break a relationship, dependent and codependent people will often experience sickening guilt when their friend, mate, lover, or parent blames them for the deterioration of the relationship. Any thought that things could be different never seems to cross their mind. The thought of altering the status quo by leaving or firmly setting limits is extremely frightening. Often they will be willing to compromise almost any personal freedom to maintain a comfort zone, no matter how destructive life in that zone might be.

In his book *How to Break Your Addiction to a Person*, Dr. Howard M. Halpern gives this sad commentary:

> Many basically rational and practical people find that they are unable to leave a relationship even though they can see that it is bad for them. . . . Friends . . . may have pointed out to them that in reality their "prison door" is wide open and that all they need do is step outside. And yet as desperately unhappy as they are, they hold back. Some of them approach the threshold, then hesitate. Some may make brief sallies outside, but quickly retreat to the safety of prison in relief and despair. . . . Something in them knows that they were not meant to live this way. Yet people in droves choose to remain in their prisons, making no effort to change them—except, perhaps to hang pretty curtains over the bars and paint the walls in

decorator colors. They may end up dying in a
corner of their cell without having really been alive
for years.[2]

At one time, if a person was chronically angry and
possessive it meant he or she had a bad temper. A person
who tried to control another's life was a busybody. If a
woman used her persuasive powers to wrap a man around
her finger, she was coy. And a man who dominated his wife
and children to the extreme was respectfully labeled
authoritarian.

But times and understandings have changed. The
bondage that has kept husbands and wives, parents and
children, pastors and parishioners, teachers and students,
friend and friend, lover and lover trapped in unhappiness
and misery has now been identified and given a name:
codependency. The most descriptive term, however, is
people addiction. And in many ways people addiction is
similar to substance addiction. Like alcoholics or heroin
addicts, emotionally dependent and codependent people
can't face breaking relationships, even if they realize they
are destructive. They obsessively hold on to a person they
know is bad for them. They also panic when they think
they will have to live without that person. This isn't the
feeling of sadness we all feel for the loss of someone close
to us; it's rather the unconsolable grief of people experiencing the loss of themselves.

BREAKING CODEPENDENCY

Emotionally dependent people who try to break out
of an addictive relationship go through the same withdrawal symptoms that substance addicts experience when
they quit drugs or alcohol. When the process first begins,
the emotional devastation is overwhelming. It feels as if the
world is falling apart. Emotions fluctuate and the individual
hopes against hope that the problem was misdiagnosed and
the whole thing can be salvaged. If the process is success-
ful and the dependency is broken, there will be a period of

mourning. Bouts of looking back, wondering what might have been, wishing for the comfort of the good times, and longing for the feelings that existed in the early days are all part of the grief experience of breaking a codependency.

Like recovering alcoholics, recovering dependents have to live one day at a time. The temptation to turn around and get right back into the codependency is strong both for the emotionally dependent person and the codependent, particularly in the first days after independence has been declared.

After mourning the end of the relationship, both the emotionally dependent and codependent individual will have a feeling of excitement and well-being—the exhilaration of freedom—because the battle for liberation was so difficult and costly. Often they will look for new and different experiences. One woman I know took up karate at age fifty. She had finally broken a codependency that had held her in bondage for thirty years. Her new sense of freedom was almost humorous as she began to find new ways to express her liberty. Sadly, some emotionally dependent people immediately stumble into another unhealthy relationship, looking for what they are always longing to find—a sense of belonging, a sense of wholeness.

M. Scott Peck described such an incident in *The Road Less Traveled*. A man came to Peck's office in despair. His wife had left him, and he claimed to be suicidal.

> "Don't you see?" he replied. "I'm nothing now. Nothing. I have no wife. I have no children. I don't know who I am."
>
> Because he was so seriously depressed—having lost the identity that his family gave him—I made an appointment to see him again two days later. I expected little improvement. But when he returned, he bounced into the office, grinning cheerfully and announced, "Everything is okay now."

"Did you get back together with your family?"

"Oh no," he replied happily. "I haven't heard from them since I saw you. But I did meet a girl last night. She said she really likes me. She's separated just like me. We've got a date again tonight. I feel like I'm human once more. I guess I don't have to see you again."[3]

The emotionally dependent person, like the chemically dependent person, has a "sense of incompleteness, emptiness, despair, sadness and being lost that he can remedy only through his connection to something or someone outside himself."[4]

We all hunger for union with someone or something to fill an incomplete part of ourselves. God made human beings with a hunger for relationship when Adam and Eve were still in perfect communion with him. Before the Serpent ever slithered onto the scene with his lying, doubt-provoking tongue, God said, "It is not good for man to be alone." And though God gave Adam dominion over all the wonderful animals he had created, still he knew that this man needed human companionship, one of the same kind. In his love, God not only offered himself as a companion, but he also created the woman. No matter what God did, however, it just didn't seem to be enough for man—or for woman.

On the day of the tragedy in Eden, the shadow of codependency was cast over our future relationships forever. Emptiness, insecurity, despair, and sadness clouded Adam and Eve's once-carefree minds. When they chose to defy the Lord God, they severed the only relationship that could make every other relationship balanced, controlled, and meaningful. They broke their intimacy with God, tainted their openness with one another, and found themselves castaway grandparents to a race of dependent-prone people. Accusations and disappointments invaded their oneness, and no doubt they questioned if being alone was not better than this.

The discontent, rebellion, idolatry, and mistrust of

our first parents have been visited on every generation with increasing furor since the day they left the Garden. And now in our time we see the full-blown effect in the dependencies and addictions enslaving our generation.

THERE IS HOPE

If you recognize even a hint of this problem in your life and if you are a Christian, there is hope of deliverance. But before you can break out of the prison of dependency, whether you are emotionally dependent or codependent, you must recognize your people addiction—an addiction that is as powerful as cocaine or alcohol addiction. Your senses are as affected as the man or woman "under the influence." You will wrestle with questions such as, "How could this happen to me?" or "How could I have been so blind?" It will be hard to admit that you have been ensnared, and you will have to struggle with your disbelief and grief before you will look for a way out.

There is a way out. To find it is to take a journey you never thought you would take. To experience it is to know beyond any doubt that in your weakness, Christ is made strong (2 Cor. 12:9). To be free is to know "if the Son sets you free, you will be free indeed" (John 8:36).

God himself has promised, "No temptation has seized you but what is common to man. And God is faithful; he will not let you be tempted beyond what you can bear. But when you are tempted, he will also provide a way out so that you can stand up under it" (1 Cor. 10:13).

No matter how long you have been trapped in codependency, there is hope for you—but it will take time!

—— JS ——

2

What Are the Symptoms of Codependency?

Webster defines the word *symptom* as "any circumstance or condition which serves as evidence of something not seen." For many people, codependency is not seen. It's merely evidenced by a characteristic behavior. It's often subtle, sometimes blatant. But to find a cure for the "something not seen," we must recognize the symptoms.

Bondage—A closeness that is appealing at first but soon turns into too many limitations on personal freedom.

Control—The ability one partner has to exercise power over the personality and preferences of the other partner.

Exclusivity—A deliberate attempt to shun the company of others and to spend an inordinate amount of time alone with one another.

Anger—The frequent expression of seething resentment that springs from slights, insensitivities, and disappointments.

Fixing—The habitual curiosity about and intervention in the partner's life, including personal habits, business arrangements, and other relationships.

Defensiveness—The unquestioned readiness to defend the relationship to all who might question the appropriateness of behavior.

Identity—A strong need to find personal value in associating or being identified with the other person.

Romanticism—An unrealistic view of what makes a healthy relationship.

Inability to choose—A paralyzing fear of choosing to leave an unhealthy situation because of the emotional consequences.

One or more of these symptoms will be present in a codependent relationship. The longer the unhealthy behavior goes on, the more apt all of the symptoms will be to manifest themselves.

As you read through the description of each symptom, don't panic if you recognize yourself or someone you love. Try to understand how that symptom reveals itself. And remember, the road to health is slow but sure.

BONDAGE

Amy was a quiet, bright, intense young woman who had few friends. She kept to herself most of the time. But when she met carefree Marie in a class at the university, she formed an instant bond. Suddenly Marie and Amy seemed to be inseparable. Marie's sorority sisters were wary of this new relationship and didn't hesitate to tell her that she was changing, and not for the better.

Marie defended the relationship and soon withdrew from the people she had been close to for two years. She and Amy moved off campus into their own apartment and created a little world of their own. They biked on weekends and studied together every night of the week. None of Marie's old friends were invited to join them in anything they did. In fact, if she could avoid them, she did. Many of her conversations with Amy were about how silly her sorority sisters were. Marie often told Amy that she was the only person who understood her. "Finally," she would say, "I have a soul mate who really understands." The mutual admiration drew both of them into euphoric oblivion. No one could challenge them without being labeled jealous. No one could be included without being considered an interruption. With every passing day, their emotionally dependent relationship drew a tighter web around them. They no longer even looked at others. Amy and Marie were in bondage to each other.

If someone who understood emotional dependency could have broken through their self-protective barrier and explained their relationship was headed for disaster, maybe they would have listened. Usually though, it takes feeling great emotional pain before codependent people will recognize their own bondage.

CONTROL

Codependent relationships form between a weak and a strong person. The strong person, the codependent, has a need to be needed, to be leaned upon, to help. The weak person, the emotionally dependent, is needy, wants to lean and to be helped. Both feel better when they operate within these roles. Each one feels good when he or she is joined with the other in a relationship. It requires so much emotional energy to perpetuate this arrangement that the two people often have little time left for other relationships.

The weaker of the two in the relationship is the one who controls it. This will come as a surprise unless you consider the logic of it. If the strong person needs to be needed, then that person will do everything possible to meet the needs of the needy partner. If the weak person complains about not getting enough attention, it will be the consuming goal of the strong one to provide attention at any cost. If the weak person has a fit of jealousy, the strong one, eager to help, will restrict the most innocent activities to keep the weak partner happy.

The following story gives a good picture of how subtly this power can work. Remember, everything can seem so right before it goes so wrong.

Ann took care of everyone. She was called the

"mother of the world" by those who knew her. She would do anything to help people. A young woman named Debbie came to Ann's church and immediately attached herself to Ann. Debbie's mother, an alcoholic, had died when Debbie was ten years old. Debbie felt cheated, and although she was twenty-seven years old, she longed to have someone who would care for her. Ann saw the young woman's need, and her motherly instincts went into motion. She drew Debbie into her family, included her in Sunday meals and holidays, and bought little gifts for her as she did for her own grown children.

Everyone seemed accepting of the situation until Debbie began to drop in on Wednesday evenings when Ann's children and grandchildren gathered for a family meal. Ann's son Robert said, "Mom, I think we need to have Wednesday nights just for the family. Could you ask Debbie to stay away?" The sense of panic caught Ann by surprise. How could she possibly tell Debbie that Wednesday nights were just for the family? Debbie wouldn't understand. Once when her sister and brother-in-law had come in from Illinois, Ann had tried to have a Sunday afternoon meal without Debbie. Debbie had cried so hard when she mentioned it. Ann comforted her, "Oh, honey, I wouldn't hurt you for anything. You just come on. There's always room at our table for you." Ann's mother-heart couldn't bear to hurt Debbie's feelings. The young woman seemed to need the mothering Ann was giving, and the friendship was very meaningful to both of them.

Now Ann really had a problem. She dearly loved her children, and if they were unhappy with Debbie's presence, then she had to do something. But she couldn't stand to devastate Debbie either.

Finally, over coffee the next Sunday afternoon, Ann told Debbie how good it was to have her as part of her family and what a dear friend she was. Then drawing a deep breath, Ann said, "But, honey, the children want me to have dinner just for them on Wednesday nights. Do you mind?''

Debbie's eyes filled with tears. She sat silently for a moment while Ann patted her hand. ''Well, Ann, if you can feel good about yourself and tell me that, then I don't suppose we are as close as we think. I'll just go now. Obviously my presence is not welcomed in this house.''

Despite Ann's attempt to soothe and to reassure, Debbie pushed by her and left determined not to be in touch until Ann apologized and changed her mind. As Debbie went to her car, Ann followed and begged her to understand.

Debbie's silence and cold stare spoke for her as she slammed her car door and started the engine. Control had just become a battleground between them. Until that point, Debbie had been in control. Ann had done whatever it took to give her the security and mothering needed. Debbie had been content—she had had what she felt she needed. Ann had been content. She had been giving what Debbie needed, and it had felt so good.

The confrontation that Sunday afternoon was the beginning of the end of that relationship. Debbie resented Ann's children and the time they spent with their mother. Ann felt like a failure. She never seemed able to gain Debbie's trust again, no matter how hard she tried.

EXCLUSIVITY

Exclusivity is a distinct mark of a codependent relationship. Because the combination of weak and strong partners makes dependent relationships possible, it's very threatening to the weaker person to contend with other personalities. Remember that the weak person is not a soft-spoken one but the one who has the greatest need to hold onto and to control the relationship. This could be the seemingly most outspoken and confident of the two. For instance, a ''macho man'' who doesn't want his wife to have relationships with other women is weak and emotionally dependent, despite his appearance and actions. Other people threaten his security. Keeping his wife exclusively for himself makes him feel more complete, more a man.

One of the most blatant and pathological forms of exclusivity is demonstrated by a man I heard about recently. When his wife told him she was leaving because he wouldn't let her out of the house to do anything on her own, he overpowered her in a rage and raped her with a cocked pistol. As he rammed it inside her, he threatened to pull the trigger. His words were all too familiar: "If I can't have you, then no one will have you." God intervened when someone came to the house and rang the doorbell. Miraculously, he withdrew. The marriage, which had been a prison-like existence, was dissolved.

I was horrified that one human being could assume such control of another's life in such a crude, ungodly way. Yet in more subtle ways, codependent relationships become islands of isolated exclusivity to which other people are not invited.

Codependent people are not free people. Freedom is the most threatening word an emotionally dependent person can hear because freedom means that the one who is stronger and more apt to have other relationships can freely interact with other people. The weaker person's exclusive rights to this loved person might have to be shared and that is too painful. Through elaborately contrived times alone, the weaker person will arrange for the exclusivity to be maintained so his or her security will be less threatened.

ANGER

Every relationship of any longevity weathers bouts of anger. Webster's *New World Dictionary* defines *anger* as "a strong, antagonistic feeling, often brought about by a real or supposed injury to oneself or others." Wherever two people interact, there is definitely potential for real and supposed injury.

In a codependent relationship, anger is always just below the surface. Resentments build as the strong person is expected to give and give to meet the demands of the weaker person. Unable to be secure and satisfied, the weak person is angered by any alteration of behavior, including changes in plans or a slight withdrawal.

Fear of losing the relationship can cause irrational responses. Childlike pleading can be alternated in the same conversations with outbursts of rage, which only escalate the resentment between both people. Although each person hates the outbursts of anger, neither of them knows how to avoid them.

Brenda and Sharon, two young executives, discovered a common interest in skiing and water sports. Since the mountains were close and the lake country was accessible, they spent most weekends together, busy with their shared interests. After about six months of this fast-paced lifestyle, Sharon, the older of the two women, began to express a need to stay home more. She felt she was neglecting her family who lived nearby. At first Brenda was understanding. But the anger within her began to rise when Sharon occasionally chose to stay home rather than go skiing.

When the two women did spend a weekend together, they spent most of their time arguing over Sharon's indifference and Brenda's disappointment. The anger began to surface regularly as they traded accusations and hard words. A simple conversation could quickly turn into a heated argument if certain buzz phrases were used. Too frequently phrases such as, "You've changed," "I can't count on you for anything," "I used to think I had a friend," and "Don't try to run my life," were exchanged.

Exasperated, weary, and frustrated, Sharon brought the relationship to an end. She felt like a failure because, as the older and stronger of the two, she felt responsible. But nothing she did seemed to appease the younger woman. Brenda avoided any contact with Sharon from that day on and asked for a transfer to another office. Six months she married.

FIXING

Codependent relationships are peopled by "fixers." They have an inordinate interest in their mate's, friend's, or child's appearance, lifestyle, dress, problems, or feelings. Fixers seem to have an uncommon need to know and be involved in every aspect of the other person's life. This can be true of both the codependent and emotionally dependent person.

Ruth Ann is a fixer. Anytime she becomes close to someone, she gets deeply involved in every intimate detail of that person's life. When she met Barbara, Ruth Ann found out about a difficulty Barbara had had for several years with her sister, Nicole. The sisters had not seen each other for several months, although they lived in the same town. Determined to be helpful, Ruth Ann called Nicole and told her Barbara's view of the problem and how Ruth Ann felt it could be solved.

Nicole was furious. Barbara was livid. Ruth Ann was puzzled. "But I was only trying to help," she said.

Fixers never see themselves as meddlesome or out of order. Their great need to help does not seem to them to be inappropriate. Their need to control and be needed is so overwhelming that they lose all objectivity. Usually they are the very last to understand that their fixing mentality is a great deterrent to healthy relationships.

DEFENSIVENESS

When our friends are attacked, we naturally want to defend them, if for no other reason than loyalty. But often codependent people find themselves in relationships they have to defend constantly. Then, defending becomes *defensiveness*. Defensiveness is a weapon used when codependent people can't bear to face the reality of their

don't like to think that their friend or mate
so much of their life could possibly be
tive influence.

ad a history of falling into exclusive, intense
with other girls. In fact, on several occasions,
her   had asked her very pointedly, "Are you
involved in a lesbian relationship?" With great rage and
even greater denial, Cindy would defend her right to love
and to be friends with whomever she wished. No matter
who questioned her, Cindy threw up a wall of defensiveness.

For several years Cindy was not involved in a
lesbian relationship, only "very intense friendships."
When she was twenty-six, her very close friend of the
moment started to rub her back. Within a few moments
they were locked in a lover's embrace. Cindy had just
fallen into the first of many lesbian affairs.

Years later, Cindy was still defending her lifestyle.
She had all of the "comebacks" that made her theology fit
her sexual preference. Armed with her well-rehearsed
answers, she quickly put any would-be concerned relatives
or friends in their place. Anyone brave enough to ask,
found Cindy unwilling to admit that her lesbian involve-
ments were anything but wonderfully gratifying and spiritually acceptable.

While all same-sex codependent relationships do *not*
end in homosexual encounters, this story is all too common
among those who search for value, significance, and
security in another person.

IDENTITY

Allison's voice quivered on the other end of the
phone. "I don't know what to do. Jim is leaving." As she
told her story, it was evident she was attached to who Jim
was, rather than to Jim himself.

The first time I met Allison, she let me know
immediately that Jim was the funeral-home director. In her

small town, that was one of the most prestigious and lucrative occupations one could have. Everyone had to die, and someone had to bury them. Jim was the only funeral director for miles around, and Allison was the only funeral director's wife.

But Jim had met a younger woman and had declared his intentions to seek a divorce and marry her as soon as possible. These are traumatic facts for any spouse to face, but the whole tenor of Allison's conversation was summed up in her whining, "I won't be anybody without Jim." Allison was threatened more than most spouses. If Jim left, she was losing more than a husband. She also was losing her identity as the wife of a prestigious man.

Emotionally dependent personalities, because they lack self-worth, attach themselves to people they esteem necessary for their existence. Such people often will be totally absorbed in another's occupation, in another's goals, in another's needs just for the pleasure of association and identity.

I knew of one young woman who had an uncanny knack for attaching herself to prominent people in a certain profession. From time to time I would hear she was in another part of the country acting as an aide to yet another well-known person. My heart always ached when I heard these accounts because she had such a consistent history of leaving behind a trail of hard feelings, accusations, and anger. Whenever the personality would no longer tolerate her clinging possessiveness, there would be a scene, and this emotionally dependent person would be floundering again to find value in herself and a reason for living.

ROMANTICISM

Everyone has a mental picture of the ideal relationship—the ideal marriage, the ideal parent-child relationship, the ideal friendship. But as we mature, most of us realize that the perfect relationship doesn't exist. However, emotionally dependent people deny that reality and believe that they can find the ideal relationship. "This time I will find the mate or the friend who will make me feel good about myself. This time, this relationship will equal those romantic, sweet scenes I've seen other people enjoy but I've never known myself."

Codependent people often promise unending security, undeniable trust, undying love, and unchangeable loyalty in the intense first days of a relationship, giving little thought of the future impact on the relationship or the possible changes that could occur. Much of the pain experienced in the destructive, waning days of a codependent relationship is created by the memory of words spoken and promises made when the ideal seemed to be possible.

One of the reasons a broken relationship is so painful for the emotionally dependent person is the crushed romantic dream he or she held to. "Here was a person who could make me feel complete." "There was a friendship that made me feel good about me." As comforting as those words sound and as reassuring as they feel, when the dream dies because of too much intensity, too many unfulfilled expectations, too many unmet needs, such words will cut to the very core of a person's being. The dream dies all too easily, and the pain lingers for what seems like forever.

INABILITY TO CHOOSE

The tears welled in my eyes as the woman sitting across from me graphically described a scene from her family's history. "My dad would come in drunk late at night. If my mother hadn't cooked dinner the way he wanted it, he would wake up my brother Bobby and drag him into the kitchen. As Bobby stood shivering in his undershorts, my father would hand him a switch and scream at him to hit my mother. My mom would cry and tell Bobby to please go ahead. I still remember the tears of rage running down his face as he switched her legs. Mom and Bobby went through with it because they knew to refuse meant beatings for both of them."

This codependent wife couldn't leave her husband. Though he beat her and her children, her codependency paralyzed her from rescuing herself or her children from his abuse. To leave was to destroy her sense of belonging. It meant her husband would be left needy, and she lived to meet his needs. After twenty-five years, she finally left. Within one year, she remarried another alcoholic. After they divorced, she met and married another. Still needy and codependent, she is searching for some place to belong, but she lacks the power to choose healthy relationships.

Codependent people feel impotent to choose for themselves in a relationship. They are so attached to the emotionally dependent person that whatever abuse is endured is more bearable than the thought of being alone. The loneliness and sense of duty bind them to destructive people and situations. It never occurs to them that they have a choice.

The relational void within each of us has a powerful impact on our decisions and behavior. Apart from union with God and an understanding of the destruction dependency can cause, your motivation to change will be very weak. Behavior that may have been part of you since childhood will not be changed unless you allow yourself to feel the pain of your experiences and see the futility of your twisted and bent thinking.

Pain is the purest motivator for change. Once you feel it, however, realize that you don't have to live this way. Begin to see that God has provided all we need to be whole. Once you see there is a way out, you will no longer be satisfied with substandard behavior.

Jesus said, "You will know the truth, and the truth will set you free" (John 8:32). Unless you know the truth about codependency, you can spend your entire life knowing something is wrong but thinking everyone else feels the same way. But, my friend, they don't. Many people who have come out of hurting, emotionally deprived, godless backgrounds can tell you that codependency is curable.

So read on. There is hope. You will get better. It will take time.

—— JS ——

3

Why Do I Act This Way?

Her words were halting but thoughtful. "To be honest about it, if I can't shake this problem, I just don't want to live."

I had only talked with the woman a few moments, but I could sense her desperation. She was ashamed to admit to me that although she was a Christian, she had not found a way to control her jealousy and possessiveness. She had made her husband a god, and her greatest fear was losing him. Every word he said was absolute truth. His opinion of her was the only opinion that mattered. His desires were always to be fulfilled at the expense of everyone else. Despite this one-sided relationship, she felt unworthy to have him because her opinion of herself was so low.

I wish her case were rare. Unfortunately, many Christians are held captive by their dependencies. The very people who support abstinence from alcohol and drugs because of their addictive nature are some of the same people who can't see their own ungodly addiction to a relationship. And all too often the problem goes on unchecked for years. Somehow it seems right and in some ways almost Christlike to be in a relationship that requires total absorption, devotion, and sacrifice—especially when one feels so unworthy.

IDOLATROUS RELATIONSHIPS

Long ago, God laid out some reasonable parameters for us to live within, and yet his people have always struggled to stay inside his guidelines. He told our ancestors that they would face some unhealthy results if they strayed from his boundaries, but they chose to wander. As a result, twisted behaviors have been manifested in the lives of the generations that have followed. God has always made his ways very clear. He has also made the consequences of straying from his ways very clear. Consider his words:

> Then God spoke all these words, saying, "I am the Lord your God, who brought you out of the land of Egypt, out of the house of slavery. You shall have no other gods before Me. You shall not make for yourself an idol, or any likeness of what is in heaven above or on the earth beneath or in the water under the earth. You shall not worship them or serve them; for I, the Lord your God, am a jealous God, visiting the iniquity of the fathers on the children, on the third and the fourth generations of those who hate Me, but showing lovingkindness to thousands, to those who love Me and keep My commandments" (Ex. 20:1—6 NASB).

Think of what the word *idol* means. Webster gives a complete definition: "an image, representation or symbol of a deity made or consecrated as an object of worship . . . the object of excessive attachment, admiration, or veneration." So when the Lord says no idols, he means nothing or no one else should be the object of excessive attachment.

What is excessive attachment? Practically stated, you are excessively attached whenever someone is on your mind constantly. If thoughts of that person keep getting in the way of your clear thinking when you try to pray, read Scripture, have a conversation, or participate in activities, then the attachment is excessive. If that person is your first and only thought when you wake up morning after morning, then the attachment is excessive. If you will not make a decision or alter your plans without considering the other person, then the attachment is excessive. If you are in constant conflict with yourself and the other person, always trying to fix the relationship, then the attachment is excessive.

Excessive attachment is *not* being in love or the natural affection you feel for a new love, a mate, a child, a beloved parent, or a close friend. Excessive attachment is an increasingly obsessive involvement with another person, with a view toward fulfilling your longing to be needed or valued. This is a choice you make to look to another person for the security, intimacy, and significance only God can give. This is idolatry, and in the end, it will reap an awful harvest.

THE VISITATION OF INIQUITY

When I talk with people about their struggles, I'm amazed at the numbers who are battling to be free of the harvest of their parent's idolatry. They say:

- My father was an alcoholic. (His idol was alcohol.)
- My mother ran around on my father. (Her idol was promiscuous behavior.)
- My father beat my mother and she just kept taking it. (Her idol was the "security" of having a husband.)
- My mother left us when we were children to live with another man. (Her idol was her own pleasure and security.)
- My father was hooked on drugs and many nights we had no food. (His idol was drugs.)

In every case, the parents were caught in an obsession with alcohol, drugs, another person, or themselves, and the children were left to cope with the "visitation of iniquity" in their own lives.

In the Old Testament Hebrew, the word for *iniquity*

literally means "perversion." It comes from a root word, *awon,* that means to "bend, twist, or distort."

God makes it clear that when the parents choose to turn from him and pursue idols, their children will experience a bending, twisting, and distortion in their lives. I believe that is one of the major consequences God speaks of when he says that the iniquity will be visited to the third and fourth generation.

> Beginning with the first sin of Adam and Eve, there was set in motion a chain reaction of imperfect parenting, through failures and ignorance and misguided actions and, worst of all, through conditional love.
>
> This parental inheritance makes every human being a victim of corporate sinfulness. We do not come into this world perfectly neutral, but imperfectly weighted in the direction of the wrong. We are out of proportion, with a bent toward the wrong. And because of this defect in our natures, our responses are off-center.[1]

I've watched with amazement as tears have welled up in the eyes of women looking for fathers who have never been there for them or who have abused and mistreated them. Without fail, these women are searching for the acceptance and approval of a father who may be long gone out of their lives, even dead. Because he was consumed with his own idols, his daughter bears the brunt of his iniquity—a bending, twisting, or distortion that has made her a target for the perversions of emotional dependency.

My heart has ached as I've looked into the eyes of young homosexuals and lesbians. Broken relationships with fathers and mothers have left them longing for a fulfillment they think they can find in a lover. A parent's idols have created a void the child desperately wants to fill. Feeling trapped, they convince themselves they were "born gay." The tragedy becomes only more tragic when the layers are peeled back and a hurting little boy who could never relate to his father cries for release, or a vibrant young woman tells of her battle to stay straight while tears flow freely for the mother who left her when she was a teenager.

I'm amazed at women who are willing to live with men without the commitment of marriage. They seem unaware that they are settling for a distortion of a God-ordained relationship in order to find the acceptance and approval they never had. But the price is very high. Abuse, attacks on self-esteem, and abandonment are only part of the cost. They also live with overwhelming guilt and feelings of worthlessness. And then there are the children who endure bending, distorting, and twisting in their own lives because their mother has chosen the idol of a live-in lover over God's law of commitment in marriage. And the generational sadness continues in a cycle that often seems hopeless.

I've been filled with anger as I have seen women continue to live with a habitually adulterous husband, enduring humiliation and rejection for occasional happiness, hoping someday he will change. But if he doesn't, she will choose to take whatever he hands out. She has convinced herself he needs her. And deep down inside she knows she needs him because she doesn't feel worthy of anyone's love. She discounts the risk of disease to her body and abuse to her heart just to feel a little security.

These women often feel the visitation of iniquity because people in the generations before them chose to go their own way and worship someone or something other than the Lord God. The thinking of these women was bent and distorted to the point that they would stay in a sick relationship just to feel needed, just to feel a little love. In their minds, God does not value them because they never felt valuable to anyone else. Seeing no way to escape and feeling deep inside that they deserve nothing better, they go through each day hurt, lonely—ignorant of a better way to live.

I'm enraged that many of these women sit in the pews of our churches, where they should be hearing the greatest emancipation proclamation of all time—the good news that we are slaves to no man, but servants of the Lord . . . who found us so precious that he chose to die for us. Somehow we haven't heard that we are free to obey God and to trust him totally with who we are and what we will become. But because our thinking is bent, some of us will turn to another person, no matter how distorted his or her thinking may be, to find the value God has already given us.

PERSONAL RESPONSIBILITY

The Hebrew word *awon* not only suggests twisted and distorted thinking, but it also suggests personal responsibility. Even though we may be visited with the iniquity of our parents, we are personally responsible for our choices and actions. If we choose evil, we must accept the consequences of our choice. Although iniquity is visited on the third and fourth generations, that generation is not released from the penalty of individual wrongdoing. "In the Old Testament, the action of man and what happens to him are presupposed to be directly related as one process within the basic divine order."[2] In other words, if any person chooses to go against God's standard—for any reason—there is a penalty inherent in that choice. The Scripture says, "For he who does wrong will receive the consequences of the wrong which he has done, and that without partiality" (Col. 3:25 NASB).

The Christian who has made choices that fall short of God's standard will face discipline. "To all who received him, to those who believed in his name, he gave the right to become children of God" (John 1:12). If we are his children, then we can expect to be disciplined. "God is treating you as sons. For what son is not disciplined by his father?'' (Heb. 12:7b). And the Scripture makes it clear, "No discipline seems pleasant at the time" (Heb. 12:11a). Although the distortion, twisting, and bending have been thrust upon the mind and heart of succeeding generations because of the sins of the parents, each of us still has individual responsibility to know the truth and straighten our thinking. That can be a difficult and arduous process.

A beautiful young woman I know lives with an abusive, unfaithful lover. She lives with him in order to escape her alcoholic parents, who dished out care and neglect equally. This young woman had every reason to leave home. But in her distorted thinking, she chose to live with a man instead of marrying him. I asked if she knew God's law about marriage. She answered, "Oh, yes." I had no doubt she was aware of violating a divine law. As much as I would have liked to excuse her in the light of the "iniquity visited on her by her parents," according to the Scripture, she is responsible for what she does with her knowledge of God. "The wrath of God is being revealed from heaven against all the godlessness and wickedness of men who suppress the truth by their wickedness, since what may be known about God is plain to them, because God has made it plain to them" (Rom. 1:18–19).

Each of us is responsible to recognize thinking or behavior that is contrary to God's standard. Disobedience will result in either penalty for the non-believer or discipline for the believer. God makes it clear we are all responsible, no matter how much iniquity has been visited in our lives. He offers the payment of our sin penalty through the death of Jesus Christ; the gift of the Holy Spirit who will lead us into all truth; and the cleansing power of his Word, which will be a light to our path. He has made a way for each of us to escape the iniquity that has been visited in our lives. So none of us has an excuse for continuing destructive behavior in our relationships. While our parents may have modeled bent, distorted thinking and behavior for us, God has given us all we need to think and behave correctly. He has clearly modeled his principles in his Word and in the life of his son, the Lord Jesus Christ.

MOVING TOWARD HEALING

As I talk with people about these dependency issues, it is my goal to show them why they are bent, distorted, or twisted and how they can move from the perversity of their situation to health and wholeness. I personally believe that if people understand why they feel, think, and react the way they do, then they can counter their thoughts with truth. If I tell a man or woman, "You are emotionally dependent because of the idolatry of your father," and then I say, "Bless your heart," excusing their sinful behavior, I have failed to offer help and hope. But if I say, "You are emotionally dependent because of the idolatry of your father, and it's sinful for you to remain dependent. But there is a way out," then I have given them information that can lead to change.

I can see no long-term value in a counseling situation in which the dependent person is encouraged to pore continuously over the details of the parents' sin. Once the transgression of the parent has been recognized and the damage has been assessed, it's counterproductive to continue discussing the parent's responsibility. The visitation of iniquity has occurred. Now the goal is to move on to forgiveness, healing, and the creation of a lifestyle in which idolatry is no longer perpetuated in any form. This new lifestyle must honor God as God and must see his laws as precious protectors for mental and physical well-being.

An important element in the healing process is coming to grips with our responsibility to extend and receive forgiveness. In his book *Healing for Damaged Emotions,* David Seamands sums up a balanced perspective about the transgression of the parents and the children's response: "The Bible makes it clear we are not merely victims. We all are sinners and share in the responsibility of who we are and what we are becoming. I have never seen anyone truly healed until, along with forgiving all those who hurt and wronged him, he also received God's forgiveness for his own wrong responses."[3]

While it's unhealthy to dwell on our parents' effect on our lives, it's also unhealthy to ignore it. It's easier to understand distorted, twisted, bent thinking if we know where it has come from. Simply to offer prayer and Bible study, as vital as they are to a person who exhibits strong relationship dependencies, is to offer tough meat to someone who desperately needs another godly person to come alongside and teach techniques of chewing and swallowing.

Paul included an appropriate model for counseling in his first letter to the Thessalonians: "Now we beg of you, please brethren, be admonishing those who are rebellious, be encouraging the fainthearted, be a mainstay to those who are spiritually weak, be always patient toward all with that patience that endures ill-treatment meekly and without retaliation" (1 Thess. 5:14, WEUST).

• • •

If you are struggling with relationship dependency in any form, I hope you can understand some of the roots to your behavior. Maybe you have come to understand that the thinking you adopted is what your parents modeled for you. You weren't born weak-willed and victimized. Your bent, because of your humanness, is toward sin. But God gives you a choice, and you are responsible for making that choice. Your behavior and twisted thinking can be changed. That's what Romans 12:2 tells us: "Do not conform any longer to the pattern of this world, but be transformed by the renewing of your mind. Then you will be able to test and approve what God's will is—his good, pleasing, and perfect will."

When you realize your life has been affected by bent, distorted, twisted thinking, there is help available. The

God who created you knows how to give light to your darkness and mend your brokenness.

> O Lord, enlighten whatever is dark in me . . .
>   strengthen whatever is weak in me;
>   mend whatever is broken and
>   heal whatever is sick in me.
> Straighten whatever is twisted . . .
>   revive whatever joy and peace
>   and life have died in me.
> Come, Lord Jesus, be the companion of my life
>   and partner for all eternity.
>
> —John Powell

No matter what kind of situation you are in, my friend, you will get better. Remember, it will take time.

—— JS ——

4

Codependency in Parent-Child Relationships

There is no stronger bond than the emotional cord that entwines parents and children. Whether for good or evil, the bond between parent and child forever influences our thinking about ourselves and our world. This is the relationship in which our feelings about ourselves are first formed and in which we first test our acceptability. It is the first contact we have with love—or a lack of it. This is the relationship that shadows our thinking and feeling about the events that happen to us for the rest of our days. Because we are tied together as part of one another's flesh, we deeply feel the pain of deficiencies and distortions in our relationship.

I've watched three bright, capable adult siblings struggle with their relationship to their mother. The oldest, Gala, is an independent, gifted businesswoman who avoids talking on the phone with her parents in a distant state. She loves her parents deeply and longs for a sense of family, a sense of belonging, but every conversation is a reminder that Gala falls short of her mother's standard. Somehow in a twisted way, their phone interactions throw Gala into a struggle with accepting herself as a person of worth.

Because she is extremely responsible, Gala is torn between a feeling that she must be the one to help her parents, should they ever need her, and a fear that she might have to spend time with them again. She is in constant turmoil. The guilt and fear that result from her mother's obvious disapproval keep Gala's feelings of self-esteem on a roller coaster.

At the age of forty, Gala is finally coming to grips

with the fact that whether or not her mother accepts her, she is an acceptable person. But in her determination to be a whole, functioning person, she has chosen to withdraw from any direct contact with her parents.

Gala's twenty-eight-year-old sister, Jill, wrote this tragic but typical letter in an effort to reach out and secure the family bond with Gala:

Dear Gala,

I'm on my lunch hour and there are things I wanted to say. But since I have a very hard time talking about them, I'll write to you instead.

There are so many things from my childhood that you don't know about. I have just in the last couple of years started to climb out of my hole and feel better about myself. Even though the three of us are all different, we are the same in a way. It has come from our home life. I can't touch it or point it out, but it was the feeling that we had to get away from home—today wouldn't be soon enough. I still feel it and despise myself and feel guilty about it, but it's there.

When Daddy was sick in the hospital, I first realized that I really did care for both of these people who are my parents. And in myself I had forgiveness and compassion for whatever they had done to make me feel so inferior for so long growing up.

The most painful time in my life was in the tenth grade, when I got pregnant. I told Daddy first. He was hurt, but I knew it would be okay. Then we went to tell Mother. That's when I wished I had died. "What were people going to think? How many others had there been?" On and on, stabbing me with words. Daddy just faded into the background as if he was helpless to help me now. Mother took over.

My boyfriend, Mike—on the verge of alcoholism—was just as confused as I was. We both needed someone we thought cared. He was so scared and immature, and so was I. But in Mother's eye, I was a total failure, and the best thing was to get rid of this problem quickly. I have nightmares of what I did. I have so much guilt for a child that never had a chance. The whole thing sent Mike into the gutter, in and out of hospitals for alcoholism. I feel responsible for him, too.

Gala, I'm not yet where I want to be spiritually or otherwise, and I may never be. But I will never give up on myself again.

Your sister and friend,
Jill

The middle child in this family, a thirty-seven-year-old named George, lives in a world of non-communication and anger. He is a hardworking husband and father. His volatile marriage stays shaky, and his only child is hostile and disturbed. Although George also hates to go to his parents' home, he still calls them every week. After every phone call, his depression rises, and the hurt he has felt so long intensifies. Although he hates the way he feels after the calls, he seems addicted to the abuse.

Each of these adult children has been pleading for his mother's acceptance all his life. Gala dealt with her hurt and need by becoming very independent and self-sufficient. She has never married and has insulated herself from the need for closeness and intimacy. The few people whom she has allowed to get past her façade know her as a very affectionate, caring woman who wants to be accepted and loved. As teenagers, both Jill and George turned to their peers for acceptance. Both married early because they had conceived babies out of wedlock. Hungry for love, they turned to anyone who thought they were acceptable, and they gave themselves totally to that relationship—body, soul, and spirit.

The mother of these three adult children is from a family of emotionally deprived people. Little affection was given, and sarcasm and conditional acceptance were a pattern of life. When she married, it didn't take long for her to turn her husband into a weak, silent observer. She probably was trying to force him to love and accept her in the only way she knew. Yet her method failed with him and with their children.

This family's story is typical. The cycle of twisted thinking and distorted behavior is passed on from generation to generation. In millions of homes, the abnormal seems normal, the unhealthy seems healthy, and men and women grow old never knowing that they can change the cycle that has gone on for generations.

Unfortunately, most people caught in these webs don't know that God has the answer for their pain and suffering. Because their behavior is so habitual, many people don't even know that what they are feeling is painful. They assume their feelings are normal. So why would they need to change? In these situations, God is rarely given a second thought unless he is used to swear by or unless he is mentioned in a religious ritual that has little relevance to life. Yet he is the only one powerful enough to bring about permanent change in the lives of people who hurt so badly.

SEARCHING FOR PARENTAL APPROVAL

Adult children who are emotionally dependent on their parents often have a deep, unfulfilled need for parental approval. One young woman I know is haunted by the fact that she never had her father's acceptance. The legacy of emptiness he left in his daughter's life is criminal. Although he is dead, she still wonders if he knows what she is doing here on earth and if he approves. She has gone from one man to another, looking for approval, yet she comes away hurt, unfulfilled, and lacking approval. The emptiness inside gnaws at her sense of well-being, and the tears of sadness cloud her eyes as she looks for ways to make herself feel acceptable. She is so emotionally dependent that she feels if only she could just see her daddy one more time and hear him say "I love you," then she could be happy.

In her excellent book about children of alcoholics, *It Will Never Happen to Me!*, Claudia Black quotes this poem, written by sixteen-year-old Renee, the child of an alcoholic:

My Daddy

I woke up one morning and he was gone
he was gone my daddy
and he would never be home again
he was gone my daddy
the one who always showed his love
the one who always understood, when she never
    would!
the one who always brushed my hair,
combed and put ribbons in my hair
he was the one who picked me up when I fell and
    skinned my knee
Oh my daddy, my daddy

I still remember all the things he taught me . . . but
    he was gone.
and I was too young to understand
she said they just didn't get along . . .
I hardly ever saw him, my daddy who was always
    there,
my daddy who always cared.
It seemed he just didn't have time for me.
But that was also ten years ago and I think now I
    understand . . .
But there's still one question that remains.
And that's . . .

Why, O Lord, did this have to happen to me?????
Why did my daddy have to go, and leave me all
    alone . . .
She says he's alcoholic, a person who has a disease
and needs help . . . but can only get it if he wants it.
He must admit to himself he is sick and needs

Help . . . She knows all this now and I do too . . .
Now it's too late, he's already gone . . .
He's remarried now and he has a new little princess
who he brushes, combs, and puts ribbons in her hair.

But Lord this is so unfair!!!
He is my daddy and he needs help!!!
But I feel so helpless Lord because it seems he still
    doesn't have time for me.
I love my daddy, whom I hardly ever see.
And even more when I think about how much he
    must love me. . . .
MY DADDY MY DADDY![1]

Whatever the reason for a parent's absence, children (no matter how old) still long to know that their mother and father love them. And they staunchly hold to the belief that if their parents ever got to know them, they would accept them. When children have not received parental acceptance, they are bound to their parents, always searching, always hoping to find a way to be acceptable.

In their award-winning book *The Blessing,* Gary Smalley and John Trent make these comments: "A study of the blessing always begins in the context of parental acceptance." For the person who has missed out on his or her parent's blessing, "Many will try to explain away and put off admitting the obvious in their lives. . . . If we never face the fact that we missed out on the blessing, we can postpone dealing with the pain of the past, but we can never avoid it. The legitimate pain of honestly dealing with this situation is what leads to healing and life."[2]

If you are a parent with grown children and if you are just now realizing that your children have never received approval and love from you in a way they could understand, it's never too late. You can still reach out to each one and say, "I'm so sorry I didn't know how to show you how loved and valuable you were and are to me. Please forgive me and let me show you how much I love you in the time we have left." Be consistent and kind, even if their response at first is a little cynical. In their heart of hearts, they want to believe you, but it may be hard for them to receive your words. Restoration may seem impossible, but it can happen.

I have a friend whose alcoholic father verbally abused her for most of her life. The father didn't like the daughter, and she didn't like him. A few years before his death, he committed his life to the Lord. His life changed so much that he couldn't do enough to show his adult daughter how very precious and valuable she was to him. Today she has sweet memories of those last years. She also credits her emotional stability to her own relationship with the Lord and those years of receiving her father's love. As long as there is life, there is hope for a change.

RESTORING DISTORTED RELATIONSHIPS

Even if your mother or father is no longer living and all hope of receiving their approval is gone, your ongoing pain can be healed. No one has to stay captive to a lack of parental acceptance. While it will be a struggle to let go and embrace the healing that is yours in the Lord Jesus Christ, it is possible. Begin to take steps now.

1. *Recognize the source of your longing.* If you have missed the esteem that a healthy parent can infuse into your self-concept, you probably feel empty, inadequate, or lonely. Because you have missed feeling accepted, the longing for their "blessing," for their approval, eats away at your feelings of worth and value. On the outside you may cover it well, but on the inside you are the little child constantly asking, "Am I okay?"

2. *Understand your behavior.* If you have a tendency toward extreme independence or excessive dependence, you may discover you have a problem feeling accepted. Think about your relationship to your parents. Did they both make you feel valued, loved, and acceptable? If not, how did you learn to compensate? Do you openly look for acceptance or do you deny your need to be accepted?

Take a quick survey of your relationships.

a. Do you find that you need to be attached to someone to feel valuable?
b. Do you find yourself being pushed away by people with whom you thought you were very close?
c. Has anyone (or several anyones) told you they need space from you because they feel you smother them?
d. Do you find yourself asking people what they think of your work or your performance as soon as it's over?

If you answered yes to one or more of these questions, then you fall into a loosely defined category of acceptance-seekers. You require overt acceptance to feel good about yourself, and you will often put up with abuse to *feel* accepted. If you answered no to the first set of questions, consider the following:

a. Do you feel distrustful when you begin to feel close to someone?
b. Do you act nonchalant when you really care?
c. Do you find a way to back away when things seem to be heading toward any form of intimacy?
d. Do you feel a certain pride in always keeping your options open so you can avoid being hurt?
e. Are you hard on yourself but feel it's important that others think well of you?

If you answered yes to a majority of these questions, you are in a category called acceptance-deniers.

The category you most resemble is really insignificant. But the answers do show that different behaviors can have the same root. Whether you seek acceptance or deny it, you have adopted some self-protective behaviors that can't cure the problem.

Take an honest look at yourself and don't cop out by

saying, "That's just the way I am!" Only when you face the reality of a root problem can you begin to find healing.

3. *Know Jesus Christ as your Lord and Savior.* This may seem like an elementary statement in the midst of all the issues you struggle with, but it's the most essential step you can take toward recovery. Since Christ is the one who makes us acceptable to our heavenly Father, a relationship with Jesus will bring security and comfort that no human relationship can bring. (If you have a question about how to have a relationship to Christ, see Appendix A, How Can I Have a Relationship to Christ?)

4. *Understand your parents' behavior.* Ask yourself, "Have my parents' backgrounds, their addictions, their personalities, or their perspective of God caused them to make parental choices that might seem perfectly normal to them? Are they treating me the way they were treated? Can I look past their actions to the little boy or little girl in them—the little boy or girl who may feel the same way I do?" Can you let them off the hook for ignorance? If you can, you will find you can be more compassionate and gentle as you interact with them.

5. *Forgive your parents.* Even if you don't understand why your parents treat you as they do, learn to forgive them. The word *forgiveness* is based on the idea of "sending away." God has said, "Vengeance is mine, I will repay." So you can be assured that justice will be done and that as a child of God you have only one responsibility: to forgive. The New Testament reminds us that when Christ was insulted, he left it to God, who judges righteously (1 Peter 2:23). You are not left as a forgotten victim. Rather, you are a powerful victor when you choose to forgive your parents for what has hurt you so badly.

6. *Tell yourself the truth about yourself.* You are a valued and loved person, even if your mother, father, or both fail to accept you.

> Though my father and mother forsake me, the Lord
> will receive me (Ps. 27:10).

Actively choose to memorize Scripture verses that tell you how acceptable you are to God, your heavenly Father.

> This I know, that God is for me (Ps. 56:9b NASB).
>
> Therefore, there is now no condemnation for those
> who are in Christ Jesus (Rom. 8:1).

The verses listed in Appendix B also will help you gain an accurate picture of who you are to God. Make a point to put these Scripture verses on 3″ x 5″ cards on your bathroom mirror, your refrigerator, and the dashboard of your car. The more you can see them and say them, the more your mind will be renewed.

You may need to say these Scripture verses out loud several times a day. Talk to yourself. Convince yourself of the truth. Give extra effort to this exercise because it goes contrary to the way you see yourself. But to bring your thoughts in line with God's thoughts is to bring health and wholeness to your mind, where the torment of being unacceptable to your parents inflicts pain.

7. *Take action.* If being with your parents brings back the old feelings of being unacceptable, do something about it. Don't continue in patterns of behavior that are painful just because that's all you've ever known. If possible, talk to your parents about your feelings. You may find that your feelings are based on misunderstanding or miscommunication. Perhaps your initiative in talking about your feelings will help your parents talk about how they do perceive you.

If talking is impossible or if it only makes things more difficult, then you do have the option to limit the time you spend with your parents. God says we are to honor our parents. You can show respect and care and yet stay away from potentially difficult situations. You are not required to put yourself through extended visits or protracted phone conversations that stir up the emotions you are working to bring under submission to the truth.

8. *Pray for wisdom.* If you continue to be haunted by feelings of restlessness or loneliness, keep taking them back to the Lord and offering them to him. You can pray something like this, "Lord, today those old feelings of being unacceptable are coming back to me. I don't want them to get a hold on me, so I yield them up to you. I give them to you to do with them what you will. I will not continue to dwell on this situation."

If your parents are still alive, pray they will know the grace and blessing of Jesus in their lives. Remember, they are probably behaving the way they have been treated, and they also need the healing touch that only God can give.

RESISTING PARENTAL CONTROL

Codependency in the parent-child relationship springs not only from lack of parental approval but also from parental control and manipulation. As the result of distorted thinking, some parents believe they own their adult children and therefore have a right to control them. Whether the parents consciously control their children or whether they do so because that's the way they were brought up, parental control can make a child's life miserable.

It's important to note that parents aren't manipulative just for the fun of it. Parents who choose this form of control often are emotionally needy themselves and are merely following a pattern learned from their own childhood. If they have failed to experience unconditional love and acceptance, if their self-esteem is flagging, if they are insecure, then they may wrongly look to their children to fulfill their needs.

At first it may be hard to recognize the problem as codependency. According to Webster, manipulation is the practice of managing or influencing by "artful skill, often by unfair tactics." These artful skills and unfair tactics take many forms. Sarcasm and continual put-downs are unfair tactics used against people who have had no opportunity to form healthy self-images. Tragically, the comments that hurt the most are often pleas from emotionally dependent parents wanting their children to fill the void they feel.

Manipulation is often softer than sarcasm and more winsome than put-downs. It can take the form of hurt feelings, tears, comments such as, "You really should have" and "If you cared, you would have." Frequent bouts of feeling bad and even chronic lateness can be very artful in controlling conscientious adult children.

Sometimes it's hard to recognize these tactics as emotional dependency because they come decorated with bitterness, resentment, and harshness. Judging by the parents' behavior, it would seem that a deep attachment is the last thing they want. But remember, dependency is spawned in an atmosphere where God is not worshiped as God, where family members have looked to substitutes to fill the deep longing of their souls, and where emptiness, loneliness, and insecurity hold them captive as they relentlessly hold to the people that momentarily give their lives meaning.

Parents who manipulate their children may never recognize this tactic as the cause of a lifetime of heartache. All kinds of people manipulate their children—sweet Christians, closet alcoholics, drug abusers, PTA presidents, and grandmothers. The older the children, the more miserable they will be as they feel the coercive pressure to conform to their parents' wishes.

Gala, George, and Jill, the three adult children mentioned at the beginning of this chapter, are the products of a woman whose sense of personal worth is zero. In her great neediness, she has tried to force them to love her—and she has failed.

This family continues under assault. Three adult children battle within themselves over the natural attachment they feel to their parents and the hatred they feel for the "artful skill and unfair tactics" that continue unabated and now are being applied to the grandchildren in an attempt to win their devotion and loyalty.

In this kind of situation, apart from the intervention of the Lord Jesus Christ, no one wins; everyone loses. The children fight the love-hate they feel. The parents feel alone and abandoned, having driven away the very people they thought they could force into meeting their insatiable needs.

STEPS FOR RESISTING MANIPULATION

If you feel as if your parent is trying to control you by manipulation, you have some choices to make. If you fail to take a stand, the difficulty will only continue and you will become a codependent to their emotional dependency.

1. *Don't let the manipulative behavior continue.* Remember that letting the controlling behavior continue is unhealthy for your parent, as well as for you. If you can hang on to this truth, then when you have to take some hard positions, it will be more tolerable to the child in you, who doesn't want to risk parental disapproval.

2. *Pray earnestly for grace, wisdom, and timing.* Harshness, coldness, and bitterness will never effect the change that is needed. You must be controlled by the Spirit of God as you deal with your parent in all the love, joy, gentleness, and patience of Christ. This will be possible only as you seek him in prayer about your hurt feelings and resentments. As he helps you identify your problems, confess them immediately and thank him that you don't have to be captive to your negative attitude. You may have

to go through this exercise every five minutes. That's okay. It will train you to give God the problems that are his and allow you to see that apart from him you really do have an attitude problem. It's a great lesson in the right kind of dependency.

3. *Reinforce yourself with the Scriptures*. Saturate yourself with verses like these:

> Do not let any unwholesome talk come out of your mouths, but only what is helpful for building others up according to their needs, that it may benefit those who listen. And do not grieve the Holy Spirit of God, with whom you were sealed for the day of redemption. Get rid of all bitterness, rage and anger, brawling and slander, along with every form of malice. Be kind and compassionate to one another, forgiving each other, just as in Christ God forgave you. Be imitators of God, therefore, as dearly loved children and live a life of love, just as Christ loved us and gave himself up for us as a fragrant offering and sacrifice to God (Eph. 4:29–5:2).

> Therefore, as God's chosen people, holy and dearly loved, clothe yourselves with compassion, kindness, humility, gentleness and patience. Bear with each other and forgive whatever grievances you may have against one another. Forgive as the Lord forgave you. And over all these virtues put on love, which binds them all together in perfect unity. Let the peace of Christ rule in your hearts, since as members of one body you were called to peace. And be thankful. Let the word of Christ dwell in you richly as you teach and admonish one another with all wisdom, and as you sing psalms, hymns and spiritual songs with gratitude in your hearts to God. And whatever you do, whether in word or deed, do it all in the name of the Lord Jesus, giving thanks to God the Father through him (Col. 3:12–17).

4. *When the time is right, calmly and lovingly talk with your manipulative parent.* Avoid anger even if you are accused and verbally abused. If you lash back in anger, you will only give your parent an excuse for his or her behavior. Kindly and firmly reassure your parent of your love. Then say that you feel controlled. Indicate that for the sake of both of you, you need to talk.

If the conversation blows up, then calmly retreat with kind reassurance of love and support. If your parent cries or pouts, don't back off, but tenderly and firmly set the limits you need to set.

Don't drag out the conversation. You will probably have to deal with it again. Be as cheerful and reassuring as possible, keeping in mind that, like you, your parent has a deep need for esteem, security, and meaning. While you are not the answer for that need, your kindness can soften the hard time your parent is going to have when you begin to pull away.

5. *Be consistent in your follow-up.* If your parent uses begging, pleading, tears, pouting, coldness or any other manipulative ploys, do not reward the behavior by giving in and backing down from your position. You are not responsible to "fix" this situation. Don't buy into the lie that if you do all the right things you will win your parent's approval and consequently end the problem. Continue to honor your parents with respect, and pray without ceasing for the grace to be firm but loving, understanding but consistent.

6. *Don't rely on your own resources.* There is no way you can handle this situation by yourself. It has taken a lifetime to develop. Only through Christ do you have the truth and the power to break out of this kind of emotional prison. In Christ, you will have the power of the Holy Spirit and God's promise that nothing will separate you from his love and that even this complex and painful situation will work together for good (Rom. 8:28, 38–39).

7. *Every time the situation comes up, take it back to the Lord.* Tell him that once again you are offering the problem up to him. Then leave it there, trusting him to guide you.

STEPS FOR PARENTS

If you recognize that you are in codependency with your children, you have taken an important step. The Lord takes great pleasure in his people who will confess their sin and admit their weakness, and he delights to repay us for "the years the locust have eaten" (Joel 2:25).

1. *Recognize that you are well on your way to winning the battle.* To recognize a problem is to make it manageable.

2. *Confess your situation.* Go to the Lord and confess (agree with him) that you are guilty of looking to someone other than him to fill the deep need and longing of your soul. Be honest with him about your own hurts and feelings from the past. You will need to go back and consciously forgive your parents and anyone else who has so wounded you that you have been hindered and held captive by your emotions.

3. *Study God's Word.* Begin an intense effort to get to know God in a personal way. As you study, ask God to teach you about his character. Come to him like a little child and ask him to give you all you need to draw close to him. Confess the longing of your soul and ask him to meet you at your point of need.

4. *Allow the Lord to fill your need.* Ask the Lord to meet your need in his time and in his way. Don't dictate how you expect him to care for you, but thank him that he is enough. This won't make you feel wonderful and give you warm fuzzies, but it will create a situation that will

train you to seek him for your needs. It's never too late, and you are never too old to seek the Lord and find that he satisfies.

5. *Ask your children to forgive you.* Confess your emotional dependency or codependency to your children. Ask them to forgive you, and if you feel brave, ask to be told whenever you slip into your old habits of control and manipulation.

6. *Involve yourself in the lives of other people who need you.* Learn the joy of giving. Find someone who is lonely, sick, or discouraged and ask the Lord to give you a ministry in that person's life. You'll be amazed at the change of perspective you can have. To redirect your focus is to free yourself from a prison that is both cramped and comfortable. It's comfortable because you have always lived there. But it's cramped because it won't allow you to be the person God intended you be.

7. *You can change.* Don't fall for the lie, "You can't teach an old dog new tricks." If you are beyond middle age, God still knows where you are and deeply cares for every burden of your heart. With the help of the Holy Spirit, you are capable of radical, life-changing alterations. It's never too late to change a situation that is deadly to yourself and to those you love.

DEPENDENCY IN OTHER AREAS

Because the roots of codependency spring from a search to fill a vacancy that only the Lord can fill in your life, discovering dependency in your relationship with your parent or with your child doesn't mean you have unearthed the full scope of the problem. Codependency is usually a learned, self-protective behavior developed from childhood in an attempt to cope with the twisted, bent, distorted thinking that has been passed on from one generation to another as a substitute for the truth. Consequently, the same behavior patterns that you hate in your relationship with your parents/children can surface in your relationship with your mate, your friend, your counselor, or your employer. The relationship can seem so right because it's familiar. Codependency can be so difficult for you to spot because you are behaving as you always have. You won't see blatant symptoms in every relationship, but all will bear some sort of ugly scar because emotional codependency is an addiction that is as harmful as any chemical addiction. Until you are able to be satisfied fully with your union with the Lord, you will battle the tendency either to take care of others to feel good about yourself or to have others take care of you in order to feel good. Neither of these tendencies is healthy for relationships.

Once you have seen the symptoms of codependency in any relationship in which you are involved, take an honest look at all other areas of your life. Don't expect to find severe dependency in every relationship, but chances are that if you are off course in your basic parent-child relationship, you may be off in your other relationships as well.

No matter what you discover as you keep reading, remember, there is hope. You will get better. It will take time.

—— JS ——

5

Codependency in Marriage

In the December 19, 1988, issue of *People* magazine, an emotional article in the "Crime" section told the bizarre and unhappy story of Peter and Patty Rosier.

At the age of forty-three, Patty discovered she had lung cancer and battled to stay alive for nine months before she and Peter made the decision to end her life by his administering a lethal dose of Seconal. Several months after her death, Peter told his story on a local television program. When the authorities heard his admission of assisting his wife in her own suicide, Peter was immediately indicted for murder.

> By all appearances, Peter Rosier was a driven man who would have done anything for the woman he loved. He and Patty had been virtually inseparable since they met as teenagers at a dance in Lawrence, New York. Patty's parents had divorced when she was young, and her mother had married Delman, a dentist, who adopted her. Peter's father was a doctor and his mother a prominent interior designer. Peter and Patty were married on March 31, 1963, while he was starting medical school. During Peter's trial, Patty's half-brother, Farrell, would tell the court, "It's as though they were one person. I don't think anyone in this room has this kind of love."

The fascination of this story is not just the mutual decision for euthanasia, but the relationship between this man and woman.

Once Patty was dead, Peter fell into a severe depression. He was barely coherent when relatives came by after her cremation to comfort him. And though he eventually stopped talking of suicide, he began behaving strangely. . . . Obsessed with Patty's memory, Peter insisted that a vase containing a fresh rose be kept at her place at the dinner table. He took up cigarette smoking, and he saw a psychiatrist regularly, sometimes twice a day.

Because they were so agonizingly lost in one another, Peter and Patty seemed to have no individual identities. A husband was devastated by the loss of his wife, and in many ways, he ceased to exist as a whole person.

Another case in the news during the same week told a story of abuse, devastation, and death. Hedda Nusbaum, a writer of children's books, an educated, articulate, once-lovely woman took the witness stand to testify against the man with whom she had lived. She told the unbelievable story of her life as Joel Steinberg's live-in lover.

She detailed abuse and emotional slavery that bound her to this man who tried to possess her soul. The ungodly situation was revealed when their adopted daughter, Lisa, was beaten to death. Hedda, looking like the loser in a prize fight, finally received the support she needed to speak out and expose the hell in which she lived.

• • •

These two stories demonstrate distorted pictures of marriage, of the relationship between man and woman. Every day couples who think they are living marriage to the fullest, with or without the sanctity of vows, struggle with their situations and wonder if there could be something better.

GOD'S PICTURE OF MARRIAGE

If asked how they would define marriage, every man and woman probably would give a different answer. Depending on experience and conditioning, definitions could range from "It's hell" to "It's heaven." So, to find a stable standard by which we can measure our perceptions, let's see how God—who created man, woman, and marriage—described this institution. He used sometimes mystical, sometimes practical words to paint his picture of matrimony.

> So the Lord God caused a deep sleep to fall upon the man, and he slept; then He took one of his ribs, and closed up the flesh at that place. And the Lord God fashioned into a woman the rib which He had taken from the man, and brought her to the man. And the man said,
>
> "This is now bone of my bones,
> And flesh of my flesh;
> She shall be called Woman,
> Because she was taken out of Man."
>
> For this cause a man shall leave his father and his mother, and shall cleave to his wife; and they shall become one flesh (Gen. 3:21–24 NASB).

There you have it—God's outline for marriage.

1. *To leave* (to separate emotionally and physically)
2. *To cleave* (to stick together like glue)
3. *To become one flesh* (to seal the relationship with the physical union)

Later God painted a practical picture no one could misinterpret when he wrote these words through the pen of the apostle Paul:

> Wives, be subject to your own husbands, as to the Lord. For the husband is the head of the wife, as Christ also is the head of the church, He Himself being the Savior of the body. But as the church is

subject to Christ, so also the wives ought to be to their husbands in everything. Husbands, love your wives, just as Christ also loved the church and gave Himself up for her; that He might sanctify her, having cleansed her by the washing of water with the word, that He might present to Himself the church in all her glory, having no spot or wrinkle or any such thing; but that she should be holy and blameless. So husbands ought also to love their own wives as their own bodies. . . . "For this cause a man shall leave His father and mother, and shall cleave to his wife; and the two shall become one flesh." . . . Let each individual among you also love his own wife even as himself; and let the wife see to it that she respect her husband (Eph. 5:22–28a, 31, 33 NASB).

God's picture of marriage is painted in crisp, two-color detail: love and respect. To see them in full brilliance is to see what God intended between man and woman—the formation of a new family unit. Marriage is to be separate from parents, bonded like glue, sealed with the sexual union, marked by the sacrificial love of a husband and the respectful submission (ranking under) of the wife.

A DISTORTED PICTURE OF MARRIAGE

Unfortunately, because of the iniquity of the first husband and wife and those of us who have come afterward, the picture has been scarred and dimmed. In his book *Love Life for Every Married Couple,* Dr. Ed Wheat states that there are three main sources of mistaken ideas about love:

1. Jumbled impressions
2. Faulty conclusions based on personal experience
3. Flawed reasoning due to cultural influences[1]

One week's viewing of American television will give accurate commentary on the marred and broken image that

we call "love." But it doesn't have to be that way. The
Lord promises that the Holy Spirit will lead into all truth
(John 16:13). And since the truth liberates, there is no
reason to stay in a state of bent and twisted thinking, even
in an age of live-in lovers, runaway mothers, and multiple
divorces. It simply doesn't have to be!

The gospel of John tells the story of a woman whom
Jesus met beside a well in Samaria, a town of half-breeds.
As Jesus rested by the well, a woman came to draw water.
He asked her for a drink, and in her coy, polished manner,
she immediately began to play word games with him. Fully
aware of her tactics, the Lord patiently talked with her
about the truth that would set her free. I believe it was to
show her the perversity of her own thinking that he said,
"Go, call your husband and come back" (John 4:16).

The woman said to him, "I have no husband" (John
4:17).

Jesus said to her, "You are right when you say you
have no husband. The fact is, you have had five husbands,
and the man you now have is not your husband. What you
you have just said is quite true" (John 4:17–18).

Here was a woman who had the facile ability to twist
the truth. She was a captive to her own understanding, and
if we could trace her childhood experiences, I believe we
would find one or both parents/grandparents failing to
honor God as God in their lives. But no matter what the
reason for her situation, Jesus offered hope and healing as
he gazed into her eyes that day. He offered her the only
relationship that could satisfy a woman so needy—a
woman who had had five husbands and a live-in lover, a
woman so needy that she would defy society to find an
answer for her neediness.

Jesus, knowing the emptiness inside her, patiently
cut through her manipulations to offer her a transforming
truth: "God is spirit, and his worshipers must worship in
spirit and in truth" (John 4:24).

When Jesus' disciples came, they were surprised

that he had been talking to a woman, but no one said anything to him about it. But the woman knew something extraordinary had happened. She went into the city and said to the people, "Come, see a man who told me everything I ever did. Could this be the Christ?" (John 4:29). As a result of what the woman said, many Samaritans believed in Jesus Christ.

I think we could surmise that this woman had never known true love for any of her husbands or for her lover. And the words "respect" or "submit" just were not in her vocabulary. She had looked for love "in all the wrong places," and in the process she had become what she never thought she would be—a sad, immoral, hurting woman.

MARKS OF EMOTIONALLY DEPENDENT MARRIAGES

Many people can identify with the plight of the woman at the well. Perhaps you are one of them. Maybe you have never been immoral, maybe you have. At this point, that isn't the issue. But the sadness and the pain of a marriage based on bent, twisted, and distorted thinking has taken its toll. You are confused and maybe despondent, and you would like to understand why.

As you read through the following list of characteristics, note which ones describe your response to your marriage.[2] I am indebted to Janet Woititz for her excellent book, *Adult Children of Alcoholics,* from which the list is adapted.

1. *You have to guess at what normal behavior is.* Because you did not see love, respect, or healthy submission exhibited in your own home, you aren't sure what a normal marriage looks like.

2. *You have an insatiable need for approval.* Because you didn't receive approval as a child, you are starved for it from your mate, who may or may not know

how to show you approval. And unfortunately, even if he or she is a master at voicing approval, you never feel satisfied.

3. *You have unrealistic expectations.* Because you are desperately looking for someone to make you feel whole, you look to your mate to give you a sense of completion.

4. *You often think about how your mate loves you rather than how you love your mate.* Because of the distortion you received from your parents, your focus is on finding someone to love you, rather than someone to love.

• 5. *You will do anything to keep a relationship intact.* Because you fear rejection and abandonment more than anything else, you will endure any kind of treatment to hold onto a relationship—especially marriage.

6. *You want to control your environment and your relationships.* Because so much of your young life was spent in a home where you were out of control, you want to be in control of what goes on in your life. (This trait makes it difficult to entrust yourself, your mate, and your marriage to the sovereign care of God—a must in loving and submitting!)

7. *Your self-esteem is very low, and you never expect to be happy.* Because you didn't experience unconditional love and acceptance from your parents, you feel unworthy to be loved just for yourself.

8. *You feel responsible for the well-being of your mate.* Because you spent your young life looking out for a mother or father who was unable to cope, it's natural for you to take on a protective, nurturing role with your mate. And you don't see this as interference with his or her ability to accept responsibility.

9. *You find it hard to trust.* Because you could rarely trust your parent to do what was best for you or to follow through on a promise, it's difficult for you to trust your mate.

All of these traits are manifested in problems with *expectations, reliance,* and *submission.* If your parents had an idolatrous relationship, you probably failed to receive "affection, clearly defined limits and respectful treatment."[3] As a result, you can expect to have some unique struggles in bringing your thinking in line with God's thinking: "Husbands, love your wives" and "Wives, submit to your husbands."

Every marriage has its share of difficulties. That's expected. But in the lives of people who are already experiencing difficulty with dependency, minor problem areas can become monumental. Learning how to strengthen your marriage is one of the healthiest things you can do, so read on with that goal in mind.

UNHEALTHY EXPECTATIONS

Lisa and Scott came from diverse but equally troubled homes. They both loved God and were well versed in the Scriptures. Although they believed that God held them accountable for their behavior, they didn't feel God loved them unconditionally.

Neither of them had ventured to have a dating relationship with anyone before they met each other. So when they met at Bible school, it wasn't long before they began to talk and pray about marriage. Soon they were convinced that it was God's will for them to marry. Both of them had reservations, but God seemed to be leading in that direction. Soon after the ceremony it became evident that neither of them could accept God's love—or each other's.

Lisa had been physically abused by a father who was long dead. When Scott tried to consummate their marriage, Lisa froze in disgust and mistrust. The marriage may have been God's will, but the physical union was nothing she could trust God with. She spurned Scott, who sank into a deep depression under the belief that he was a failure, just as his parents had always told him he would be. The first fires of intimacy, for which Lisa and Scott both yearned, were quickly extinguished. They left school disillusioned with one another and with God.

• • •

Emotionally dependent people have unrealistic expectations for the role a mate can play in their lives. Starved for closeness and a sense of belonging, the emotionally dependent person sabotages intimacy by often demanding more than any human can possibly give.

Intimacy, which arises from close personal connection, is the glue that holds marriage together. For the person who missed a sense of being connected to one or both parents in an intimate way, marriage seems to be the answer to emptiness and low self-worth. Wanting intimacy is a valid longing within each of us. However, for the emotionally dependent person, it is more than a longing— it is an obsession. For the codependent, it is a duty to pursue.

In her book *Struggle for Intimacy,* Janet G. Woititz writes about the unrealistic expectations of people from dysfunctional homes.

> Those who are products of homes where bonding never took place, if they invest at all, invest at once, heavily and on a deep emotional level. They seize the opportunity for bonding and are deeply involved before they know what is happening.
>
> In the early stages of a relationship, there is great intensity of feelings. The body chemistry that attracts you to each other is activated, and both parties are super-attentive and super-involved. . . . This is the time when both parties greatly desire fusion. You are on each other's minds all the

time—the phone calls are frequent—the desire to be together is great. Emotionally, it is a very powerful time.

You cannot sustain this intensity which is so appealing. This is just a dynamite beginning, and not what a healthy relationship is all about.

Initially, this is flattering to the partner, and the closeness feels good. Often the partner gets pleasure out of feeling needed and in fulfilling the needs of the other love object. But after a while this begins to feel suffocating, and starts to become a drain. Your partner, if healthy, will stop wanting to be devoted completely and exclusively to the relationship. Life holds other priorities, as well. The aura of the ideal love evaporates as a result, and things begin to be put into perspective.

When life begins to normalize, the intensity decreases. . . . You feel let down and rejected. From your point of view, this feels like abandonment. . . . Clutching at your partner will force him/her into the "I love you, go away" stance, even though your beloved still cares. If you continue to play out your script, you will set yourself up for what you fear the most: rejection and abandonment. Then you will feel very confused because all you wanted was a loving relationship, and you will think . . . you picked the wrong person. The truth may be that you were asking unrealistic things of your relationship.[4]

It can be a shocking realization to find that the very things that were appealing in your spouse's personality have become abhorrent to you. Initially you avoid admitting that there is a problem, but you can't avoid the problem forever. That's why I'm so compelled to get the information in this book into the hands of every struggling man or woman. There are healthy ways to face the problems of codependency, and I believe the initial step is *recognizing the problem*. When you dare to recognize your problems and have enough courage to believe that God is bigger than your difficulties, then you are on your way to healing.

UNHEALTHY RELIANCE

Many people assume that when they get married, they will be able to rely on their mate to be strong in the areas where they are weak. Ideally, two people complement one another when they join together to form a unit.

When God created Eve out of Adam's side, he was making a helper for the man—a woman to whom Adam could stick like glue and a relationship he could honor with the sexual union. Together they could meet one another's needs, replenish the earth, and even be a picture of the coming Messiah and his church (Gen. 2:18–25; Eph. 5:31–32).

When sin entered the picture, the marriage relationship became twisted and distorted. Needs became exaggerated, the mental image of sticking together like glue became more accurately symbolized by a ball and chain, and fidelity became infidelity—overnight.

And through the years, marriage for many has become an escape for those starved for parental affection and esteem. Some who were codependent escaped to become care-takers, others, who were emotionally dependent, escaped to be cared for—and often they have found each other.

Ellen is a caring, compassionate, and confused young woman. She has a beautiful face, lovely hair, and she knows how to apply just the right touch of makeup. Ellen is also 150 pounds overweight.

When we first met, Ellen was depressed because her husband had moved in with another woman. As her story unraveled, a pitiful cast of characters played out their roles in the drama of her life.

Her parents as well as her husband's parents were concerned but very critical and volatile. Ellen spent most of her conversations with me telling of incredibly insensitive acts on their part. Once when Ellen and her husband had been in an automobile accident, Ellen was seriously injured. Her husband was unhurt but very drunk when the rescue squad arrived. While he leaned over the car, waiting for the jaws of life to extricate his wife from the wreckage, his father drove up on the scene, jumped out of his car, and started screaming at the rescuers for tearing up his son's car. He cursed his bleeding daughter-in-law, yelling, "If you weren't so fat, they wouldn't have to ruin the car."

When I expressed my outrage at this whole ungodly scene, Ellen merely shrugged her shoulders and said, "Oh, well." She was too weak to stand up for herself and confront the people who abused her. She was too fearful that her two daughters would be taken away if she made a fuss.

Ellen's weakness made her a sitting duck for her husband's weakness. She wanted to be loved and cared for, but she married a man who constantly put her down. Because he needed to feel superior, he married a woman he could abuse.

I asked Ellen why she stayed with a man who was adulterous and abusive. Her answer was expected. "He needs me, and I guess I need him." While the circumstances vary with every couple in this kind of marriage, the characteristics are the same.

In her excellent book *Growing Closer,* Dr. Marie Chapian writes about "Starvers" and "Providers":

> Dependency is destructive when we seek to find ourselves in somebody else. You are dependent as a Starver because you crave the constant approval and support of another person. You are also dependent as the Provider, because you must have the dependency of the Starver in order to feel worthwhile. Both of these roles are filled with frustration and dissatisfaction.
>
> Nobody benefits by weakness. Feeling powerless creates a need to please in order to feel secure. Trying one's wings, daring to fail, and taking risks are too threatening to a person whose

security is shaky. The irony is that such dependency upon others for approval breeds hostility and resentment toward those depended upon. It is not uncommon to resent the one you most desperately want to be close to. These feelings can be compounded by guilt because, after all, the person is so good to you.[5]

When marriage is the union of two needy people looking for fulfillment in one another, it fails to fit the biblical picture God has drawn of mutual support, love, and respect. It becomes instead a garish cartoon of people trying to be real but never finding a way because each one's "realness" depends on attachment to the other person.

UNHEALTHY SUBMISSION

Submission has been the battleground between men and women since the Fall. When economic power was totally male dominated, women often were forced into roles of subservience by their inability to provide for themselves and their children apart from a husband. In far too many situations, men's power corrupted, and women led lives of physical and emotional abuse that in no way resembled God's picture of married love. Consequently for many women, the choice to rank herself under the protective, nurturing headship of a loving husband was unheard of. Her lot, instead, was to give whatever her husband demanded of her because she needed to be cared for. It never crossed her mind that her role was one of voluntarily limiting her behavior for the well-being of her husband and her marriage. She never saw herself as a valued partner, standing beside him to make their union stronger.

Today things have changed economically; women can make it on their own financially. Some Christian women have come to understand the difference between duty demanded and service volunteered. Many women, however, live in the mystique associated with being totally subservient to a man. Many emotionally dependent women choose to take the physical abuse and emotional assault of an unfaithful spouse because they are afraid of what life might be without him. These women are too insecure within themselves to believe that God would value them enough to say, "This is not submission."

Remember that many men and women have come out of homes where God was not honored as God and where the parents were dysfunctional or absent. These men and women have had no models of normal married life. They have difficulty trusting each other. They have deep needs for approval, and they often exercise great control over one another. Apart from the powerful intervention of the Lord Jesus Christ, many marriages become a living hell. And the flames flare the highest in the battle over submission.

In her book *In the Name of Submission,* Kay Marshall Strom quotes a woman caught in a typical problem: "After my husband beat me severely for the third time in a month, I turned in desperation to my minister. I wish I hadn't. First, he assured me my husband was not a bad man and meant me no harm. Then he instructed me to be more tolerant, more understanding, and to forgive my husband for beating me, just as Christ forgave those who beat him. I went home determined to do better, but I was greeted at the door by a punch in the face. How much must I tolerate? Does Christ really want me to stay in an abusive situation?"[6]

Strom then asks the question, "Does God's word condone the kind of blind submission and subjection that can logically lead to the battering of wives by their husbands?"[7]

The issue goes even deeper because most, if not all, women who would have to ask that question are probably struggling with a need for approval. They feel "I'm not worth any more than this" and "God expects me to take this kind of abuse because I probably need to be punished."

Add to this mixture, "I need this relationship to be happy. If I submit to anything, I won't lose this person on whom I depend for everything." There you have the distorted, twisted, bent thinking—so far from God's standard, so far from his picture of marriage.

WHAT IS NORMAL?

God has sketched the outline of a marriage picture in his Word. He has made broad, full strokes as he graphically described what marriage is to be.

> Leave
> Cleave
> Become one flesh
> Husbands, love
> Wives, submit

Then God permits the man and woman to fill in the colors and shadings of their own personal outline. Each union will be different. In fact, every marriage should be different because of the myriad of personalities that are coupled together. But the foundation should be standard.

Let's look at a few of the differences between emotionally dependent marriages and emotionally stable ones.

Codependent Marriages	*Interdependent Marriages*
Expectation	Expectation
1. That emotional intensity will be sustained.	1. That intensity will fade comfortably.
2. That there will be emotional support on every level	2. That mate won't meet all emotional needs—no one can.

3. Exclusive devotion.

3. Other friends, other interests.

4. Security is based on undying commitment and promises.

4. Security based on personal inner strength and relationship with the Lord.

Reliance

1. "I need my mate to be happy. Without him/her, I'm not a whole person."

1. "I can be happy as an individual. I'm complete in Christ."

2. "I don't deserve happiness, so anybody I get will be acceptable."

2. "I don't have to seek happiness in a relationship that is mostly painful."

3. "If I don't look out after my mate's happiness, who will?"

3. "I'm not responsible for my mate's happiness, although I want to give unselfishly of myself to bring joy to him/her."

4. "If he/she doesn't love me, then I'm not loved, which proves my belief that I am unlovable."

4. "Whether or not my mate loves me, God loves me, and I will be loving toward my mate."

Submission

1. "I need to control my wife, and she must obey me."

1. "I'm the leader in my home, and I need to lead and love my wife as Christ leads and loves the church."

2. "I have to submit to my husband no matter what. Even if he abuses me, I will submit."

2. "I choose to rank under my husband's leadership out of respect for him and in obedience to God."

   a. "This is what God expects."

   a. "This is pleasing to God."

b. "I don't really de-
   serve any more."

b. "This brings order to
   our home."

RESTORING CODEPENDENT MARRIAGES TO INTERDEPENDENCE

If you recognize yourself on the dependent side of the chart or if you see that you have an unhealthy perspective of the foundational elements of marriage, don't be discouraged. There is hope. If you really want to find the wholeness and freedom that God intends for you, then begin to take these steps toward healing.

1. *Call your problem by name.* Verbalize the truth. Say, "I have some unhealthy dependencies on _____." Saying the words helps you see the urgency of your situation.

2. *Confess.* Go to God and confess (agree with him) that your dependence is not in line with his will. Admit that it is sin. God clearly states in 1 John 1:9, "If we confess our sins, he is faithful and just and will forgive us our sins and purify us from all unrighteousness." God promises two things:

a. He will *forgive*. Once you have confessed, you are free of the load of guilt you bear when you are living short of God's mark.
b. He will *purify* from all unrighteousness. That means he gives you a new beginning. He will wash away the stain of your sin, and he won't keep bringing up the failures of your past.

3. *Pray for guidance and strength.* You'll need to make many changes in your marriage relationship. Ask God to guide your decision making and to strengthen your courage to do what he shows you.

4. *Trust God*. Don't expect the changes to be easy. But when the going gets rough, remember who you are in Christ and all that he promises to do for and through you if you will just allow him to. (Read Appendix B, "Your Value in Christ." If you are not a Christian, then please take the time to read Appendix A, "How Can I Have a Relationship to Christ?")

5. *Be accountable*. Ask the Lord to give you someone—a mature friend or counselor—to whom you can be accountable. Old habits and faulty thinking are hard to break. It helps to be accountable to someone who knows you and loves you but who also will confront your thinking in order to bring about the changes you need.

6. *Work on your relationship to the Lord*. Spend time with him each day, reading his Word and pouring out your heart to him. He is the only one who can satisfy your need for intimacy and for emotional support. He is the only one worthy of your unquestioning obedience. Your relationship to him will be the source of right thinking and right action.

7. *Pray for wisdom*. When you don't know what to do, ask the Lord. The Scripture reminds us, "If any of you lacks wisdom . . . ask God, who gives generously to all without finding fault" (James 1:5).

8. *Find healthy role models*. Spend time with people who have healthy, godly marriages. If you don't know any personally, read about them in good books. One of the most precious stories I know is told by Dr. Ed Wheat in his book *Love Life For Every Married Couple*.

> A man loved his wife tenderly and steadfastly for a total of fifteen years without any responding love on her part. There could be no response, for she had developed cerebral arteriosclerosis, the chronic brain syndrome.

At the onset of the disease she was a pretty, vivacious lady of sixty who looked at least ten years younger. In the beginning she experienced intermittent times of confusion. For instance, she would drive to Little Rock, then find herself at an intersection without knowing where she was, or why, or how to get back home. A former school-teacher, she had enjoyed driving her own car for many years. But finally her husband had to take away her car keys for her safety.

As the disease progressed, she gradually lost all her mental faculties and did not even recognize her husband. He took care of her at home by himself for the first five years. During that time he often took her for visits, she looking her prettiest although she had no idea of where she was, and he proudly displaying her as his wife, introducing her to everyone, even though her remarks were apt to be inappropriate to the conversation. He never made an apology for her; he never indicated that there was anything wrong with what she had just said. He always treated her with the utmost courtesy. He showered her with love and attention, no matter what she said or did.

The time came when the doctors said she had to go into a nursing home for intensive care. She lived there for ten years (part of that time bedfast with arthritis) and he was with her daily. As long as she was able to sit up, he took her for a drive each afternoon—out to their farm, or downtown, or to visit the family—never in any way embarrassed that she was so far out of touch. He never made a negative comment about her. He did not begrudge the large amount of money required to keep her in the home all those years, never even hinted that it might be a problem. In fact, he never complained about any detail of her care throughout the long illness. He always obtained the best for her and did the best for her.

This man was loyal, always true to his wife, even though his love had no response for fifteen years. This is agape, not in theory, but in practice!

I can speak of this case with intimate knowledge, for these people were my own wonderful parents. What my father taught me about agape love through his example I can never forget.[8]

This is the kind of relationship we all long for. If we should be blessed to have a mate who loves us with an agape love—unconditional love—that is wonderful. But agape love is not something you can expect, demand, or make happen. The only power you have over agape love is to give it to another person. Marriage is the institution in which this kind of love is best demonstrated. So when you marry, you have an opportunity to give the highest and the best. But you must remember, you can't expect it.

• • •

If you have been in pain because you have bought into the belief that your needs must be met and you must be loved unconditionally, then there is hope for a new perspective.

You will get better. It will take time.

—— JS ——

6

Codependency in Friendship

The friendship of two men brought tears to the eyes of theater patrons several years ago when the movie *The Killing Fields* was released. And what a classic story of friendship it was! Two strangers—one Western, one Oriental—met and together experienced the communist overthrow of Cambodia. They shared days of danger and deprivation, never knowing what would happen next.

When their final hours together came, a sense of despair filled the theater as the two friends were separated. And in the center of despair was the hurt of realizing that the American, Sydney, could have gotten his Cambodian friend, Pran, out of Phnom Penh before it fell. Sydney acted in his own interest, and as a result, Pran was unable to leave when Sydney left. Pran was left behind to fend for himself during the hellish downfall of Cambodia.

Sydney returned to his accolades and journalistic awards in the West, but he hated what he had let happen to Pran. Sydney became obsessed with finding Pran and rescuing him. Pran survived his ordeal, clinging to the hope that one day Sydney would come.

After years of desperate searching, Sydney received the news that Pran had made his way out of Cambodia and was in a refugee camp in Thailand. Sydney left New York immediately to retrieve the friend he had left behind so long ago.

Only the hardest of hearts could hold back tears as the two friends saw each other for the first time after painful years of separation. As the two men embraced, Sydney looked into Pran's eyes and quietly said, "Forgive me?" With the loving trust of a little child, Pran said, "Nothing to forgive, Sydney. Nothing to forgive."

The audience had just been eyewitness to the highest and noblest in friendship: self-sacrifice, loyalty, forgiveness, and trust.

WHAT IS A FRIEND?

Everyone needs a friend. Some of us need many friends, while others are content with few. But we all need friends.

Throughout the centuries, people have tried to express the value of a friend:

> What is a friend? A single soul in two bodies (Aristotle).

> A friend is one attached to another by affection or regard (Webster).

> Fate chooses our relatives, we choose our friends (Delille).

> A friend is one who walks in when the whole world walks out (Walter Winchell).

> A friend is someone who would take a great risk for me, someone I could call at four in the morning and say, "I need you to help me bury a body," and he'd come with a shovel, no questions asked.[1]

> Two are better than one, because they have a good return for their work. If one falls, his friend can help him up. But pity the man who falls and has no one to help him up! (Eccl. 4:9–10).

Each of us has an ideal of friendship in our mind. Your description may be different from your friend's, but the relationship is always founded and maintained on loyalty, self-sacrifice, forgiveness, and trust if it is really to be called a friendship.

BIBLICAL PICTURE OF FRIENDSHIP

God gives us a biblical model of friendship in the story of David and Jonathan. Their relationship held together through days of separation, family interference, threats, danger, and in the end, Jonathan's death.

What enormous pain must have flooded David's heart as he wept for his beloved friend!

> "How the mighty have fallen in battle!
> Jonathan lies slain on your heights.
> I grieve for you, Jonathan, my brother;
> You were very dear to me.
> Your love for me was wonderful,
> More wonderful than that of women" (2 Sam. 1:25–26).

Surely as David poured out his grief, his mind went back to the field where he and Jonathan had come together and had entered a covenant with one another. No doubt his heart convulsed as he remembered hiding in the bushes, waiting for Jonathan to tell him if he needed to flee from Saul. And with stinging tears, I'm sure he thought of their final embrace as they left each other for the last time—David to become a fugitive and Jonathan to return to the house of his father, Saul.

No words could adequately describe David's loss. Jonathan was dead—the most self-sacrificing, loyal, trustworthy friend a person could have. The same friend whose final words still rang in his ears: "Go in peace, for we have sworn friendship with each other in the name of the Lord, saying, 'The Lord is witness between you and me, and between your descendants and my descendants forever'" (1 Sam. 20:42).

What a picture of godly friendship! What a union of the heart we all long for! It is part of our humanity that we desire soul-linkage with others who will make us feel more competent, more sufficient, more complete and unconditionally loved.

HEALTHY FRIENDSHIPS

R. J. Sternberg, in his paper "Measuring Love," written for Yale University, cites these core needs in friendship:

1. To be able to count on the other person
2. To feel mutual understanding
3. To get emotional support
4. To value one another
5. To want the best for each other
6. To feel happy in each other's company[2]

Healthy friendship fulfills the deep longing within each of us to be able to trust, to be understood, to be supported, to be valuable, to have someone in our cheering section, and to feel likable. When friendship works the way God intends it to, it provides all of this and more. Each partner "strengthens the hand of the other in God." Each is stronger for having befriended the other. Unfortunately though, many friendships turn to bondage and sadness. Emotional dependency kills and destroys what God intended.

Healthy friendship is based on interdependence, which means two people are equally dependent on one another. This quality is vital to solid friendships. They must be borne out of mutuality. God made us to have friends, to depend on one another, to enjoy the bolstering that a friend can give—to be interdependent.

CODEPENDENT FRIENDSHIPS

In her book *Among Friends,* Letty Cottin Pogrebin says,

> We want friends we can depend upon, and in turn, we also pride ourselves on being the rock in someone else's storm. But the cloying, draining, energy-sucking friend is not a thing of beauty and a joy forever. The ties that bind can also strangle.

Dependency is a suffocating form of enclosure. And weakness can be a powerful tool for manipulation in the hands of the friend who is incessantly needy or inconsolable, the one who keeps escalating the crises that require your intervention, and the one whose daily conversation resounds with cries of "I'm falling apart." However faint the voice, such pleas can be as coercive as a shout.[3]

This is the type of relationship that can't go unnoticed. This is the relationship that breaks the commitment of the strongest and destroys the will of the most determined.

WHAT CAUSES FRIENDSHIPS TO GO WRONG?

Friendships deteriorate for many reasons. Let's examine several characteristics of codependent friendships.

CONDITIONAL ACCEPTANCE

When we first enter a friendship, we do so because we are attracted to the other person. Our acceptance of that person is based on attraction: we like what we see.

But what happens when we begin to see the other person's flaws and phobias? It's easy to say "I love you just the way you are" when the attraction is still vibrant. But when we are being hurt because our friend is insensitive or uncaring, suddenly it's not so easy to be accepting.

Or what happens if we were attracted to the other person for the wrong reason? In his excellent book *Quality Friendship,* Gary Inrig warns, "Friendship is built upon mutual attraction, but there is a problem with attraction we must notice. We can be attracted to others because of a lack of love in our lives. We may see the other person primarily as someone who can meet our needs. Such a negative basis can have devastating results."[4] And the results become evident when the person to whom we are attracted fails to meet our needs. When that happens, we begin to question the acceptability of that person. As we see the flaws and phobias of the one to whom we were attracted, disappointment overwhelms acceptance.

In relationships built on deep emotional need for acceptance, small situations will be blown out of proportion. Soon both friends will begin to ask what's wrong with the relationship. When this happens, we will start to talk about things that need to change "to make this a good relationship" or "to make things the way they used to be." It's as if our needle gets stuck in one groove, and we can't get out of it. Every time we talk to our friend, dissatisfaction creeps in, and neither friend is really happy anymore. Something is always wrong. As we look to a friend to meet our need for nurturing, the whole situation will get more volatile as the disappointment mounts.

The idea of having lifelong needs met is very attractive. The tragedy is that one person, no matter how loving or determined, can never fill those requirements. Eventually the attraction will dwindle. When the sizzle and warm fuzzies are gone, then the acceptance becomes conditional: "I will be your friend only if you meet my needs." Dependent relationships are built not on mutuality and respect but on an atmosphere of "I will be everything to you forever—no matter what."

UNREALISTIC EXPECTATIONS

People from dysfunctional homes, where parents have failed to deal with one another and with their children in a healthy way, have only vague ideas about what is "normal" in relationships. Consequently, they have a tendency to develop unrealistic expectations in friendships.

Because they were not nurtured, they may look to a friend for nurturing. Because they have low self-esteem, they may look to a friend to provide positive reinforcement and affirmation to build self-esteem. Because they received little approval, they may look to a friend to lavish approval and praise in greater amounts than normal.

Healthy friendship naturally provides some nurturing, esteem, and approval. But emotionally dependent people may place on a friendship expectations that go beyond any one person's ability to fulfill.

These unrealistic expectations frustrate both people in a relationship. Soon they both feel disappointed, hurt, and empty. One person may try to force the other person into meeting certain expectations, but he or she soon learns that you can't force a friendship to be what you expect it to be! All you can do is live up to your own ideals of being a friend, without placing high expectations on the other person. You can't buy friendship or create it. You can't demand it or expect it.

CONTROL

Emotionally dependent people feel the need to control what happens in the friendship. They can't stand the thought of letting this person get away when he or she has such a significant place in their life. The codependent person works overtime to keep the emotionally dependent person happy—after all, his reputation is at stake. Whether their need is to be a caretaker-fixer or to be cared-for-and-fixed, codependent people try to control the relationship to meet their own needs. For the emotionally dependent person who already has low self-esteem and insecurity, it is difficult to abandon control and allow the codependent to be free. Control becomes a very delicate and potentially volatile issue.

Many people assume that the controlling person will be the stronger of the two. That's not necessarily true. Weak people can be very adept at controlling friendships. Consider the friend who uses, "Please love me," as a response when a discussion gets heated. Think about the person who says, "But you said you would always spend special time with me," when it's inconvenient to meet as planned. Notice the effect of the friend who says, "If you loved me, you would have been there," when plans had to be changed at the last minute.

Although the statements sound weak, they're really quite strong. They give a "you-should-have" message that is hard to handle. The emotionally dependent person's goal is to get the friend in line—and often it works. Guilt is a powerful taskmaster. When we care about another person, we don't like to hear that our actions, no matter how innocent, have hurt our friend. And if we are codependent, emotionally when we hear the pitiful cry of the dependent person, it's tough to be objective. We want somehow to make the relationship better. Often we will go against our better judgment to appease. When that happens, we have allowed ourselves to be controlled. Eventually we will become disgusted with the needy friend and with ourselves. There is just no way to win in a codependent relationship.

In her excellent booklet *Emotional Dependency,* Lori Thorkelson Rentzel lists some ways emotionally dependent people try to control other people.

- *Finances:* combining finances and personal possessions such as property and furniture; moving in together
- *Gifts:* giving gifts and cards regularly for no special occasion, such as flowers, jewelry, baked goods, and gifts symbolic of the relationship
- *Needing Help:* creating or exaggerating problems to gain attention and sympathy
- *Time:* keeping the other's time occupied so as not to allow for separate activities
- *Pouting:* brooding, cold silences; when asked "What's wrong," replying by sighing and saying, "Nothing."[5]

For a while, the battle for control goes undetected, but eventually one of the friends realizes that the relationship is producing guilt when there is no reason to feel guilty. The relationship becomes a struggle rather than a friendship. Eventually one of the friends will try to break free, and unless there are massive changes within the heart of each person, the friendship is over.

JEALOUSY

Webster defines *jealousy* as "mental uneasiness due to suspicion or fear of rivalry." When a friendship is based on great need for approval, esteem, and security, anything or anyone who is viewed as a threat can create jealousy.

Mental uneasiness creates incredible torment for the threatened person in the relationship. Suspicion of every motive and every move will cause strange behavior. Otherwise ethical people will open mail, listen in on phone conversations, follow a friend's car, drive by a friend's house, and actually try to trap the friend.

Chuck Swindoll describes jealousy in these graphic words: "Like an anger-blind, half-starved rat prowling in the foul-smelling sewers below street level, so is the person caged within the suffocating radius of selfish jealousy. Trapped by resentment and diseased by rage, he feeds on the filth of his own imagination."[6]

Jealousy works hand-in-hand with rage and anger. It's impossible to hide the mental uneasiness. Probing questions, prying behavior will soon cause the whole relationship to erupt. No friendship, no matter how stable, can survive this kind of assault.

AMBIVALENCE

Because codependent relationships lead to bondage greater than anyone can ever imagine, ambivalence—mixed emotions—will eventually surface. Most dependent friendships start out exceptionally well. In fact, that's what is so fascinating and fun about them. But that's also one of their weakest points. Codependent relationships often start with the assumption that "This will be the friendship that will give me a sense of wholeness. This is the bonding that nothing can break. Let's form this friendship as quickly as possible.'' Dependent relationships are built not brick by brick, but wall by wall—often much too quickly to be lasting.

When the problems begin, disbelief sets in. The memories of the good times in the early days tip one side of the scale, while the pain and bickering of the present tip the other side. When the friends remember the good times, their feelings are positive. When the frustration of the present surfaces, their feelings are negative. The interesting thing that seems to happen in codependent relationships is that the scales never tip for any length of time toward the positive. The friends may feel positive for a short time, but once things begin to go wrong, the fun is gone, the freedom is gone—and so is the peace.

It should be evident at this point that no friendship can endure for long under these conditions. Yet people hungry for esteem, love, security, acceptance, and approval will hang on in desperation, thinking, ''It's going to get better.'' While some codependent relationships can be repaired, the vast majority are casualties because the price for health is often too high.

PREVENTING CODEPENDENT FRIENDSHIPS

What can you do now to prevent your friendships from becoming twisted by emotional dependency and bent by codependency?

BEWARE OF TOO MUCH TOO SOON

In her booklet *Relationships,* Pamela Reeve says, ''The most common problem in relationships is that of moving into depth too quickly. Proverbs 12:26 puts it well: 'A righteous man is cautious in friendship.' He moves slowly. He doesn't over commit himself. Making friends slowly is basic to good relationships.''[7] For the dependent person who is either hungry to be needed or who needs to be cared for, a friendship can be the most exhilarating, intense experience of a lifetime.

The promise of being loved, known, understood, and accepted is too good to be true—and too much to wait for when the void for love is so deep.

One man has said that a friend is a person "who knows all about us and loves us just the same." We all crave that kind of security in a relationship. But for the emotionally dependent person, the deep need to be "loved just the same" exceeds the boundaries of the best of relationships. Acceptance is romanticized and often hastily pursued with disastrous consequences.

DISCUSS AND ESTABLISH LIMITS

When you first become friends, the mutual attraction and positive feelings seem to preclude the need for setting limits. One of the most positive things you can do, however, is to communicate early on what is acceptable to you in the relationship. If you sense the potential for becoming a codependent in a relationship, then you need to set limits and talk them over with your friend. This can be done graciously and with sensitivity. But if you have experienced the agony of being entangled in a codependent friendship, you won't shy away from taking this precaution.

ESTABLISH ROLES

Sometimes it's necessary to say how you view the roles in the relationship. If you sense your friend might become emotionally dependent, then talk about roles in a healthy relationship. Remember, not everyone enters a friendship knowing what "normal" is. You need to be aware of what roles will bring disastrous results. It's better to define healthy roles early on and avoid the pain later.

Dr. Marie Chapian gives good advice in the area of establishing roles in friendship. I have heard her say over and over as she has addressed conflict in relationships,

"Remember, you are not one another's mother, psychiatrist, or pastor."

Friends can't assume the role of mother for one another. If you do, you take on more responsibility than you ever bargained for. You will also find you will encounter more hostility than you ever counted on. In reality, no one wants another mother. Although a friend can meet certain "mothering" needs, in the long run a relationship based on that kind of nurturing will not last.

Friends can't assume the role of psychiatrist for one another. At first it may seem worthwhile and even entertaining to try to figure out one another and make suggestions for change. But sooner or later it gets old. If acceptance is vital to healthy friendship, then it's counterproductive to analyze your friend's idiosyncrasies and phobias, especially with a view toward bringing a change. It's just not a friend's job.

Friends can't assume the role of pastor for one another. Nothing will sour quicker than a friendship in which one friend assumes responsibility for the spiritual growth and training of the other. I'm not speaking of a formalized relationship of disciple-teacher; I discuss the issue of discipleship in chapter 8. Instead, I'm referring to friendship in which one friend uses Scripture, prayer, and sermonizing to try to alter the behavior of the other. There is no mutuality in this kind of relating.

If you are wise, you will establish roles early in your relationship. As you discuss your roles, ask yourself these questions:

- Do we differ in age?
- Do we differ in need?
- What are your expectations for depth and intensity?
- Do I have other relationships—marriage, family obligations, other friendships—that need to be considered as I establish my role as friend with this person?

- Do I want another friend?

These questions should not be left to work themselves out. You will save pain and time by clarifying these issues in the beginning.

ESTABLISH LIMITS ON TIME AND INVOLVEMENT

If you have a tendency toward being a codependent, you might want to say:

- "I can see you during the week for lunch from time to time."
- "I can't talk with you on the phone at night because of my family."
- "I would love to talk to you before 11:00 any night."
- "Weekends are study time for me. I know you understand."

Although these statements make a relationship seem very structured, they will help you avoid misunderstanding that will rip your heart out later. In friendships that develop slowly over time, these issues may resolve themselves without discussion. But in important, intense relationships, discussing these limits is vital, especially if you become friends with a person who, due to emotional dependency, either wants more than you do or who wants to cling to you for security.

ESTABLISH LIMITS ON RESPONSIBILITY

Again, if you tend toward being a care-taking codependent, learn to say:

- "I'll keep your dog anytime."
- "Sorry, I just don't co-sign bank notes."
- "Just call me if you need me."
- "I'll do whatever I can, but you'll understand if family responsibilities come first."

Misunderstanding about what you can expect from a friend can be devastating. To avoid conflict and upset, discuss what you are willing to be responsible for. It's better to start out conservatively rather than promising the world and then finding yourself having to back up in the face of a demand. Be realistic. Ask yourself what you can legitimately give in this relationship. You may want to give more, but time, money, and other obligations may keep you from being the ever-present, faithful helper you might desire to be. If that's the case, deal honestly with yourself and your friend.

BEWARE OF JEALOUSY

If you perceive any tinge of emotional dependency, you might say:

- "Friendship is so important to me that I really won't allow us to be jealous of one another."
- "I love you enough to allow you freedom to do or be whatever God has enabled you to do or be. Don't ever let me interfere by being possessive or jealous."

No one plans to be jealous. It creeps in unexpectedly and often takes root before you know what has happened. If you will determine beforehand that the first sign of jealousy on the part of either friend will be ruthlessly dealt with, then you will have established healthy guidelines for your friendship.

ESTABLISH OPEN AND HONEST COMMUNICATION

Whether you tend toward being emotionally dependent or codependent, communication is essential:

- "I love you."
- "I have a difficult time with my feelings when you tease me about my weight."
- "I need some time by myself today. Let's plan for lunch tomorrow."

● "Would you forgive me for forgetting your birthday?"

Learn to talk openly and honestly. Learn to take one another at face value, and determine not to read between the lines or put words in one another's mouth. Friends should be able to talk with candor, no matter how touchy or volatile the situation could be.

ESTABLISH A SPIRITUAL BOND

If you tend toward codependent relationships, a spiritual bond can be refreshing. Just beware that it can be counterfeited as a spiritual bond when in reality it is codependency. Remember, this is a subtle addiction that can come in through many windows. Just be sure the primary conversation is about the Lord, not your relationship.

● "I will pray for you."
● "What has God been teaching you?"
● "Did you read that passage in Isaiah? What do you think?"
● "There's a Spiritual Growth Conference next week. Do you want to go?"

The deepest, most satisfying relationships are those founded on a mutual love for the Lord and desire to grow in him. There is no greater bond than the one between two people who love one another enough to "strengthen each other's hand in God."

My Friend, beware of me, lest I should do
The very thing I'd sooner die than do—
In some way crucify the Christ in you.

If you are called to some great sacrifice,
And I should come to you with frightened eyes
And cry, "Take care, take care. Be wise, be wise!"
See through my softness then, a friend's attack,
And bid me get me straight behind your back.

To your own conscience, to your God be true,
Lest I play Satan to the Christ in you!

And I would humbly ask of you in turn
That if someday in me love's fires should burn
To whiteness, and a voice should call
Bidding me leave my little for God's all—
If need be, you would thrust me from your side
So keep love loyal to the Crucified!''

—author unknown

CURING CODEPENDENT FRIENDSHIPS

As with any addictive behavior, codependency is far easier to prevent than cure. Once you have started to relate in an unhealthy way in a friendship, it often takes radical surgery to bring about health.

Awareness is the first step toward healing. If you have identified any of your friendships as dependent, then you can choose whether you will look for some answers or remain in an ever-tightening bondage. The answers are not the same for every friendship. Some are easily repaired when both friends realize what has happened. Often, however, the entanglement is so complex that it takes strong medicine plus a miracle from God to restore or create a healthy relationship.

If you think one of your friendships needs attention, try these antidotes:

1. *Recognize and emphasize your value to yourself and God.* No one survives a dependent relationship without personal devaluation. No one likes to feel unworthy, unloved, or incapable of meeting a friend's needs. So whether you are the emotionally dependent friend or the codependent friend, you're in a no-win situation. Learn to feel good about yourself and absorb the great, forgiving, unconditional love of God.

2. *Recognize the value of the moment.* In dependent relationships, the emphasis often shifts to "what was" and "what could have been." Learn to focus on the present, on what you *can* do now.

3. *Recognize that security is found only in God.* People die, people fail, people walk away. That's the reality of life. The reality of God is that he will never leave or forsake you.

4. *Give and receive freedom.* Recognize that giving and receiving freedom is the most effective medicine to cure dependent friendships. Give each other space and fresh air. Talk about freedom. Remind one another to focus on freedom. Insist on freedom.

Pamela Reeve comments in her booklet *Relationships,*

> The word "friend" comes from the Old English root word "freon"—to love, akin to "freo"— free. I must leave the other free, free to be herself. I must allow her to have her own feelings, think her own thoughts, do things her own way, make her own decisions. If I don't, she will feel she is being swallowed up and losing her own identity. Her alternatives are to either succumb to a destructive relationship or to withdraw.[8]

5. *Ask God for wisdom.* Many Christians in codependent relationships pray often, but they focus on the life, character, and behavior of the friend. This is normal and natural as long as the relationship doesn't begin to dominate your prayer life, your time in the Word, and your outside reading. The consuming nature of a codependent relationship can easily do that if you are not aware of the subtle hold it has on your life.

If you want God's wisdom, ask in childlike humility. Ask him to purify your thoughts and motives as you pray about your friendship. Ask him for wisdom that will supersede your own neediness or your own guilt. Ask him to show you clearly and specifically what you are to do in relation to your friend and your friendship. When you believe he is giving you direction, compare it to the description of wisdom in James 3:13–18.

> Who is wise and understanding among you? Let him show it by his good life, by deeds done in the humility that comes from wisdom. But if you harbor bitter envy and selfish ambition in your heart, do not boast about it or deny the truth. Such "wisdom" does not come down from heaven but is earthly, unspiritual, of the devil. For where you have envy and selfish ambition, there you find disorder and every evil practice.

> But the wisdom that comes from heaven is first of all pure; then peace loving, considerate, submissive, full of mercy and good fruit, impartial and sincere. Peacemakers who sow in peace raise a harvest of righteousness.

6. *Ask God to work in your life.* Ask the Lord to pull up the roots of dependency. Be determined that this will not be a recurring pattern in your life.

   a. Seek Christian counseling that will help you develop godly and healthy relationship skills.
   b. Get into a Bible study that will teach you how you can study and apply God's Word for yourself. (I think *Precept Upon Precept* Bible studies, available through Precept Ministries, Box 221822, Chattanooga, TN 37422-7218 are the very best!)
   c. Read Christian books that will reinforce your skills in a practical way and help you clarify your thinking. (An excellent book is *Telling Yourself the Truth* by William Backus and Marie Chapian.)

d. Get involved in a church that works as a body, one in which every member is important and involved and the Word of God is honored as alive, powerful, and applicable to your life today.

7. *Be willing to sever the friendship.* When it becomes evident that your growth and freedom will continue to be stifled, be willing to end the friendship. This is the most difficult and radical cure of all. Yet when the clear evidence indicates that this situation not only is going to continue but also is decaying, radical action is necessary.

For the emotionally dependent person, severance can be worse than death. The perceived rejection can be unbearable. As hard as it is, my friend, this is the soil in which God works best to draw our dependencies to him, where they belonged in the first place.

For the person who has been the codependent fixer-caretaker, ending the relationship is devastating too. The feeling of guilt can be overwhelming. Questions such as, "How could I possibly have failed my friend?" keep popping up to torment you. Although you will hate to let go, you'll find this situation is a great school for learning to trust others to God's care.

Broken relationships are not what God is all about. He is a redeemer, a reconciler, a mender of broken hearts. But sometimes he has to break so he can heal. He has to separate so he can teach. He has to intervene so he can bring understanding.

If one of your friendships is decaying or has already ended, then you understand the pain involved in this kind of action. It hurts. For the believer, however, Christ injects a promise into this kind of painful, heart-rending situation:

> "A bruised reed he will not break, and a smoldering wick he will not snuff out" (Isa. 42:3).

> "Do not fear, for I am with you;

> Do not be dismayed, for I am your God.

I will strengthen you and help you;

I will uphold you with my righteous right hand''
(Isa. 41:10).

My friend, never forget, you will get better. It will take time.

7

Codependency in the Workplace

Shortly after her graduation from Bible school, Judy came to work for Muriel as an administrative assistant. Judy is a hard worker and devoted to Muriel's work with inner-city children. Judy is now thirty and still single. Although she would like to marry someday, she has discouraged any would-be suitors by her rapt attention to the children's work and Muriel's needs.

The last two years have been extremely painful and fraught with conflict for these two women. Because of growth in her work, Muriel has added two other staff members to her organization. Each woman has met an icy welcome from Judy, who has been passively cooperative but emotionally sensitive since the other two have joined Muriel. Judy frequently complains of feeling left out and of being replaced. She does her work well but has become increasingly reluctant to tell anyone, including Muriel, about her procedures for her filing system. "I'll get you anything you want," is the stock reply she gives to all questions.

Because she and Muriel were the whole staff for several years, Judy built a real mother-daughter-friend closeness with Muriel. Because Judy's mother was an alcoholic and very distant, Judy viewed Muriel as the mother she felt she never had. Muriel enjoyed having an adult to care about since her life's work was with children under the age of twelve. Judy worked beside her during the day and spent countless evenings at Muriel's apartment, watching television and just hanging around. They both seemed to enjoy the arrangement.

When the work load increased, Muriel felt trapped. She knew that hiring another worker would cause all kinds of problems with Judy, but eventually she had to do it. She tried to pave the way for the situation by taking Judy with her on a trip to Florida, but once Muriel told her that she was hiring more workers, Judy clammed up and didn't respond to Muriel through the rest of the trip.

Now, two years later, the conflict has been constant. Judy has good days and bad, although she seems to have a lot of headaches, misses work more frequently than before, and is easily offended. Muriel feels trapped because Judy has become like family to her. Judy has stood beside her, worked far beyond what was expected, and yet is so hurt by the current situation. Muriel has rearranged the working situation four times in two years, but nothing seems to please Judy. The two new employees have both told Muriel they didn't know how much longer they could work there because Judy was so difficult. Muriel feels frustrated, angry, guilty, and manipulated. She hates it, but she wonders if she will ever find a way of escape. She feels such an obligation to Judy.

•   •   •

Codependency affects the workplace just as it affects parent-child relationships, marriages, and friendships. It's easy to get caught in dependency without knowing it because the symptoms don't show up in the beginning. The eagerness, the commitment, the dedication on the part of the employee, and the understanding, sympathy, and charisma on the part of the employer make for a "honeymoon" period that is frequently astonishing to both employer and employee.

However, tiny cracks begin to show in the relationship when the first pressure comes along to threaten the status quo. As was true in Judy's case, change is the most threatening situation an emotionally dependent person can encounter. If the pressure lasts long enough (and it usually does), the cracks will grow deeper, and the work environment will be profoundly effected.

EFFECTS OF CODEPENDENCY ON EMPLOYERS

Supervisors who are hooked into codependent relationships will react in some of the following ways:

1. *Employers will refuse to confront the employee.* Confrontation, no matter how gentle or deserved, often brings a flurry of defensiveness and upset from the worker. As a result, the employer may leave work undone rather than face an emotional scene with the employee. If the relationship started out well, the employer may have let down his or her defenses in an attempt to build a relationship. But if difficulty arises, the employer may feel guilty about confronting an employee who is so close.

2. *Employers will reverse plans for restructuring if the employee complains.* Change always brings strain. In the work force, change is usually met with some sort of resistance. But for the employee-employer locked in a dependent relationship, change can bring so much stress that the employer may back down from plans for change because of the employee's complaint. This reaction hurts the company and the other employees. Dependent relationships can turn an otherwise strong boss into a helpless, ineffective leader who feels trapped by the dependent employee.

I have seen this happen in organizations that have gone through the growing pains of moving from a small "we're-all-family" company to a corporation. The problems come when the dependent employees, who find their esteem and value in being part of "the family," are threatened with the inevitable changes. If the managerial staff bows to the outspoken maneuvering of these employees, growth will be stymied and the employees who could make the greatest contribution may often be set aside for the emotional needs of the others.

3. *Employers will route work to someone else in order to preserve the peace with the dependent employee.* When a relationship is dependent, the supervisor often can't bear, or many times just gets tired of, the effort it takes to keep the dependent employee pacified. Remember, an emotionally dependent person has a big problem with being out of control. If change or unwanted work is introduced into this person's environment, the only way the employer knows to control it is through pulling emotional strings with anger, sadness, disappointment, and the "poor me's."

EFFECTS OF DEPENDENCY ON EMPLOYEES

Employers can expect emotionally dependent employees to express some typical behaviors:

1. *Employees will sabotage change.* Dependent employees will drag their feet in learning new procedures. They will express their displeasure with the system every time they have an opportunity.

2. *Employees will appear to be extremely self—sacrificing.* In an attempt to manipulate their bosses, emotionally dependent employees often work late and come in early to "get the job done." This kind of sacrifice will never be done in silence. Employees will make sure everyone else knows about their hard work. It becomes their trademark. People will comment on their work and tell them, "I don't know how you do it." With resolute determination, dependent employees will shrug and say, "Someone has to do it." But in their hearts they think, "I'm the only one who can do it, and the boss knows it." Happy to have such a devoted employee, employers will praise the employee's dedication. What employers often

don't see is that they are controlled by the emotionally dependent employee. Actually, the boss is becoming a codependent, but how can a boss not give in to an employee who works so hard?

3. *Employees require a great deal of attention from the boss.* Emotionally dependent employees will create a lot of questions, problems, and "impossibilities" that will keep the boss attentive to the situation and ever aware of the significance of these employees.

4. *Employees will use emotions to manipulate.* Emotionally dependent employees will use moodiness, pouting, and outbursts of anger to control not only the boss but also other workers. Dependent employees make themselves appear to be so valuable that people around them feel as if they have to walk on eggshells.

THE EMPLOYER-EMPLOYEE RELATIONSHIP

The interaction in a codependent work relationship is complex. More is at stake than the smooth running of the workplace. The self-esteem of two or more people is under siege.

The employer wants to be valued as a good boss, particularly by an employee who has shown such devotion and self-sacrificial dedication to the job. The employer, therefore, avoids or diffuses every encounter that might create a change or bring a blowup with that employee.

The employee often feels inadequate unless he or she has the employer's attention and appreciation. The employee often will do anything to get that attention. "Anything" includes sweetness, helpfulness, working overtime (even at the cost of one's own private life, including spouse and children), as well as emotional outbursts, pouting, crying, and habitual illness (even though the employee still comes to work).

In such a wide spectrum of reactions, it's very

difficult to know what is real, imagined, permanent, or temporary. Consequently, the employer who finds esteem in being liked and fiercely supported is puzzled about what to do with a devoted and dependent employee.

STEPS FOR HANDLING DEPENDENCY IN THE WORKPLACE

1. *Recognize that you have a problem.* Admitting the problem is always the significant first step that eventually will lead to recovery if you really want to effect change.

2. *Realize that the basic issue is esteem.* When personal value is derived from a job or an accomplishment, then anything or anyone who changes or threatens that job becomes an enemy to be outwitted by any means one can muster. Esteem is that sense of being regarded highly because of an innate value. It also can be explained as "acceptance garnished with appreciation." For emotionally dependent people who spend their lives looking for acceptance and approval that they somehow missed in their formative years, the workplace becomes a laboratory for experimentation in how to win, manipulate, or steal what they have always longed for.

3. *Take responsibility for your own actions.* If you find you are tiptoeing around subordinates because they are prone to scream, cry, pout, or be harsh if you cross them, take a reasonable, responsible look at what is really going on. You are being controlled. You are allowing it to happen, and you are doing nothing to create an environment for healthy work relations. If you sit back and take an objective look, you'll discover you aren't the only one being controlled. Others, perhaps with less rank than you have, must order their conduct according to the behavior of the controlling, dependent person. If the one who is in charge plays into this situation, then the other workers are

helpless to effect change and are victimized by the behavior of the emotionally dependent employee.

4. *Take stock of your own emotional health.* Are you afraid to take charge of a dependency situation because you fear losing approval and appreciation? Be honest. Is your esteem on the line if this person—who has served beside you, sacrificed long hours for you, and has gone well beyond the call of duty—is upset with you for confronting inappropriate behavior? If it is, could you be dealing with a codependency on your part? Realize that even if you consider yourself the stronger (by virtue of your position or temperament), you are being manipulated if a person can get positive strokes from you by inappropriate behavior. The weak is controlling the strong. You can make the choice not to reward manipulative behavior.

5. *Assign individual responsibility.* The employer must assume responsibility for "giving in." The employee must assume responsibility for inappropriate behavior. This will not be a sweet time. Anger, frustration, panic, and threats will fill the air. But once the confrontation is over, the situation will improve if the employer is firm and consistent.

6. *Set acceptable parameters.* Define what behavior is appropriate in your situation. Then set up guidelines for yourself and the employee. Once you have set the behavior code, deal with any breach as soon as it occurs. Old habits are hard to break. So confront every infraction kindly and consistently.

7. *Ask God for insight, wisdom, and a sustained desire to correct the situation.* Ask him to show you any blind spots you have and thank him that he is the Redeemer who does not leave us stranded in our messes.

CODEPENDENCY IN CHRISTIAN MINISTRY

Be aware that Christian ministry is not exempt from emotional dependency. In fact, the opposite is true. Christian ministries often are led by appealing, charismatic people whose very temperament and personality attracts dependent people. Ministry, then, often becomes the perfect setup for codependencies to surface.

Because the results of codependency can be so devastating, Christian leaders need to be aware of the symptoms and dangers. Great wisdom needs to be exercised in hiring personnel or taking on volunteers. Often leaders are so thrilled to have help that they are blinded to the potential danger of an emotionally dependent person attaching themselves to the ministry in order to meet their great need for acceptance and approval. Since Christian principles are based on tenderheartedness, kindness, forgiveness, and patience, dependent people often take advantage of these characteristics. They grab hard and hang on tight to the leaders, hoping to feel good about themselves—perhaps for the first time in their lives. Emotionally dependent people hope to gain esteem from identification with a strong personality. And warm-hearted leaders can find themselves codependent before they realize what has happened.

BEWARE THE GREATEST DANGER OF ALL

He is a pastor in a very prominent church in a large northern city. I had heard his name mentioned many times as I traveled in Christian circles, but I had never met him. His wife called me one night after she attended a conference where I had been speaking.

"We need help. And we're willing to go anywhere to get it."

"Sam is entangled with another woman, and he desperately wants to get out. Right now, they are just seeing one another. She volunteers as a secretarial assistant in the church office. He knows he is in danger. He has come to me and confessed the whole thing, but he feels trapped. The other woman is begging, pleading, and even threatening to expose him.''

''Please, can you tell me where we can get help?''

I took her number, called her back in the morning, and arranged for them to go out of state to see someone I believed could help.

I would like to think that this situation is rare. Unfortunately, I have heard and seen too much. Not only is it far too common in the secular marketplace, but it has invaded the church as well. Seemingly innocent needs become passions almost overnight.

Wherever there is a strong, charismatic personality who seems self-assured and competent, there will be people who want to identify with that person to bolster their own lack of esteem and personal value. There are two common ways to get such a leader's attention. Offer to help in any way you can or ask for help with your needs. Either way, you can catch the unsuspecting with the hook of either ''You need me and I can do a lot for you because you're so busy'' or ''I need you and you can do a lot for me because I'm so needy.''

The workplace, whether secular or Christian, is a fertile field for codependent relationships to grow into infidelity. The proximity, the everyday contact, the frequent opportunities to talk are all nourishing for relationships. For the dependent person and for the one who needs someone to depend on him or her, it too frequently opens a door to tragedy. The cycle is rather commonplace. Unfortunately, it reads like a soap opera:

''I need someone to understand.''	''I understand you.''
''I need more time to talk.''	''I'll give you time.''
''I feel so alone.''	''I'll hold you. I'm here.''
''I need you to hold me again.''	''Of course I will.''

"I've never known anyone like you."	"Really?"
"I need to talk. I know it's late."	"I'll be right there."
"I never meant for it to go this far."	"I didn't either."
"I think we shouldn't see each other."	"I can't leave you."
"What if your wife (or husband) finds out?"	"We haven't been getting along lately anyway."

It all begins with a genuine desire to meet a legitimate longing. And when it's all going on, it seems so right because feelings are being soothed, value is being restored, and longings are being fulfilled in both lives.

To have the need to be loved and accepted is not sin. To have a genuine desire to feel acceptable and approved is not sin. To look for a fulfillment of those needs begins to border on the dangerous. But to allow the need to overshadow your sense of righteousness and to violate God's law is sin. James 1:14–15 warns, "But each one is tempted when by his own evil desire, he is dragged away and enticed. Then, after desire has conceived, it gives birth to sin; and sin, when it is full-grown, gives birth to death."

No one wins when needs are met in an ungodly way. Adultery has never ended in anything but death to relationship, death to a good conscience, death to trust, death to dreams and hopes, and for the Christian, death to effective ministry.

I can remember a memorable lesson taught by Wayne Barber, pastor of Woodland Park Baptist Church in Chattanooga, Tennessee. His three points, which focused on the adultery of David and Bathsheba, never left me, though it has been years since I first heard them:

1. Sin will cause you to *stray* farther than you ever intended to stray.
2. Sin will cause you to *stay* longer than you ever intended to stay.

3. Sin will cause you to *pay* more than you ever intended to pay.

CODEPENDENCY AND HOMOSEXUALITY

We spend a lot of time in the workplace. For many people the communication and understanding they share with fellow employees is far greater than what they share with their families. Because of the time factor and the opportunities to communicate on a deep level, there is often a temptation for homosexual and lesbian encounters. Whether in the secular marketplace or in Christian ministry, the same potential exists. No matter where it occurs, it is a tragedy of monumental proportions when people use illegitimate and ungodly means to fulfill their need to be accepted, secure, and understood.

One woman claims she was first seduced by a nurse in a hospital. The woman was lonely, needy, and dissatisfied with her husband. The nurse took an interest in her and began coming to her room to meet her emotional needs. After the woman left the hospital, the nurse continued to check on her. Soon they were drawn to one another, and before too many months passed, they were locked in a torrid lesbian affair.

This whole series of events started over twenty years ago. I hear from the woman occasionally as she cries for help, claiming she is sick of her life. Sometimes she is living alone; other times she has taken up with another lover. She knows the truth. She has made commitments to Christ, but she is so addicted to lesbianism that she can't see she has already strayed, stayed, and paid more than she ever thought she would—and all the consequences have not unfolded yet.

STEPS TO AVOID ILLEGITIMATE EMOTIONAL ENTANGLEMENTS

1. *Turn from evil.* Determine to live by the biblical injunction to "abstain from every form of evil" (1 Thess.

5:22 NASB). I've often heard people say, "No matter what I do, someone isn't going to like it. Why shouldn't I just do what I want to do and be happy?" A statement like that reveals a person who has not yet realized the great sacrificial love of Christ, who willingly died to save us from evil, and all the pain and devastation it brings. There is nothing good about "abstaining from evil" on the inside but playing with the appearance of it on the outside. The two are incompatible wherever they are found. Look at your own situation and answer the following questions. Let your answers put boundaries on your activities.

    a. Will it appear evil if I work late with a co-worker of the opposite sex as the only other person in the office?

    b. Will it appear evil if I go to lunch alone with a co-worker of the opposite sex?

    c. Will it appear evil if I hug my secretary/boss?

    d. Will it appear evil if I rub my boss's shoulders?

    e. Will it appear evil if I _____ ?

You fill in the blank. Self-examination that is candid and objective is a healthy step to wholeness. If you have doubts about any activity, then avoid it. What may seem perfectly harmless to you could give the wrong signals to a friend or co-worker. In her book *The Snare,* Lois Mowday, a vibrant young widow, relates an experience that gives light to this subject.

> A few years ago I was at a convention attended by many Christians from around the world. It reminded me of the many wonderful times my husband and I had had at such conventions in the past. The atmosphere was upbeat and fun.
>
> Many of the men were there without their wives. I was finding it increasingly difficult to deal with my feelings of loneliness and wondered how some of the men who spent weeks away from home handled this problem in a godly fashion.

I saw an old and trusted married friend sitting in the lobby one afternoon and asked him to join me for a cup of coffee. He did and we talked of his ministry and mine. We discussed the fact that he had been away from home for five weeks and that I had been widowed for several years. With no hidden agenda in mind, I asked him how he handled loneliness. Because it was time for the evening meeting, he suggested we meet afterwards to talk. I agreed, with only a slight feeling of uneasiness.

After the evening session, we met in the lobby, and he abruptly led us out of our hotel. He hailed a cab, and we left for another spot to get a cup of coffee. A red flag was waving in the back of my mind, but I kept ignoring it. Part of my reasoning was because this was a trusted friend and Christian leader, and another part of it was because it felt so good to be out after 9 P.M. with a man!

I loved this brother dearly, but was not physically or emotionally attracted to him. We went to a nearby cafe, and in the course of the next twenty minutes, it became obvious to me that he had more in mind than talking. He immediately backed away when he saw that I was shocked and had no intention of doing anything but talk. We went right back to our hotel, and he politely left me in the lobby by the elevator.

When I got to my room, I was filled with mixed emotions. There was disbelief, excitement, confusion, disgust, and a wonder about what might have happened if I had pursued his suggestion.

Why did this happen? I asked myself that question over and over. What had I done to give the impression that I wanted something "physical"? At first, I couldn't think of anything.

Then I remembered that *I* had initiated the invitation to have coffee and that *I* had asked the question about loneliness. I had not considered his state of mind at that time. He was alone, and had been so for weeks. We were good friends, and he didn't know if I was attracted to him or not.

Of course, my feelings, one way or the other, did not make his approach right, but *I* was the one who started the ball rolling with my provocative question. Having coffee with him in the afternoon in our hotel coffee shop wasn't wrong. Asking him a pressing question wasn't wrong. Having coffee with him late at night away from the convention was very risky, and continuing the discussion about the provocative question was wrong and unfair.[1]

2. *Be ruthless with yourself.* If you realize you are in a dependent relationship with another person, whether of the opposite or same sex, start to back off. Codependency is the first step toward personal and professional disaster. If you are a trusting, loving person, you may be naïve about the background and experience of a co-worker. One woman nearly fell into a physically intimate relationship with another woman in her office. She felt uncomfortable with the hand holding and long, drawn-out hugs, but her friend and co-worker convinced her nothing was wrong. "Our conduct is perfectly harmless," she insisted. At that point the uncomfortable person followed her instinct and backed off. Don't go against your convictions. They will protect you when your emotions are not dependable.

3. *Don't create a problem in the mind of the other person.* If the relationship has just been fantasy for you, then deal with it by yourself and with the Lord. Don't put your notions into the other person's head, or you may get into deeper waters than you planned. Consider the following comments:

From a Christian counselor after a conversation with a woman in his congregation: "A woman came to speak to me to tell me that she had a strong attraction for me that she knew she should not have. My first response was, 'What have I done to make her feel like that?' My second response was an 'ego' response, which made me more interested in why she felt as she did. This could have set up the wrong set of dynamics for an ongoing relationship. Her expressing of her feelings to me created a difficulty for me to work through. In looking back, it created more of a problem for both of us than if she had not ever expressed it."

From a Christian businessman who was close to his pastor: "My pastor told me that a woman in the congregation had come to him and admitted to having fantasies about him. He, in turn, told his wife. The result was that his wife developed neurotic behavior that damaged and undermined their ministry in the church. It would have been better had he not communicated that statement to his wife."[2]

4. *Ask the Lord to purify your heart and mind.* As you go to the workplace each day, ask the Lord to put a hedge of protection around your mind (Job 1:10) to deflect Satan's fiery darts, which come in the form of sensual or suggestive thoughts (Eph. 6:16).

5. *Study God's Word.* Keep God's Word as a first priority in your life. "For the word of God is living and active. Sharper than any double-edged sword, it penetrates even to dividing soul and spirit, joints and marrow; it judges the thoughts and attitudes of the heart" (Heb. 4:12).

6. *Change your behavior.* The proof of your recognition of a real problem will be changed behavior. The degree of dependency you have on the other person will determine the degree of change needed. You may be able to detach yourself emotionally if you stop seeing each other altogether. It may even be necessary to leave your job. If your relationship is too entangled (physically and emotionally), the only way to get out is to cut the strings and separate.

Don't excuse yourself if you are only emotionally involved. Remember that emotional involvement is the first step in the process that leads to immorality.

If the other person knows about your feelings for him or her, tell the person that you realize the relationship is wrong and that you are going to change your part of it. Tell the person firmly but gently that you can no longer have personal conversations, that you will relate to him or her only on business. It is important to resist trying to convert the person to your point of view. Just say how things have to be—and go.

If the person questions your change in behavior, answer as briefly as possible in a matter-of-fact way. Be kind but avoid lengthy conversations. Discussing the problem will only keep the relationship going longer than is desirable.

If the relationship has been sexual, stop seeing the person immediately. To continue seeing a person with whom you have been physically intimate is keeping temptation too close at hand.

After you have broken off a relationship, you will be very vulnerable. Guard your emotions carefully. Develop new activities and relationships to help you resist the temptation to return to the unhealthy relationship.

If your dependency on a person of the same sex has led to homosexuality or homosexual thoughts, these suggestions from the booklet *Homosexual Struggle* may help.

1. It is important to see unhealthy relationships as sin and to view them in the light of God's truths.
2. Talk with someone who is willing to listen patiently without giving pat answers.
3. Stay away from tempting situations.
4. Be willing to endure loneliness while allowing God to change your life.
5. Refocus your attention. Think on things that are true, honorable, right, and pure

(Philippians 4:8) and "set your mind on things above" (Colossians 3:2) rather than on the person or situation, which is not in God's will for you.[3]

• • •

I pray that if you see yourself in this chapter, you will run to the arms of Jehovah-Jireh, the all-sufficient one who can give you the strength, wisdom, and fortitude that you will need to pull yourself away from a relationship that can only bring tragedy to you.

Again, I remind you. You will get better. It will take time.

8

Help! I'm Dependent!

If you have come to recognize that you are an emotionally dependent or codependent person, what are you going to do about it? If you recognize that your relationships need to change, what are you going to do?

Facing the process of change can be very painful. Your emotions are difficult to live with. The pain of codependency is like no other. The bondage of being addicted to a person, the fear of losing the relationship, and the panic of being swallowed up by the needs of another person create excruciating pressure.

A Christian caught in dependency discovers double misery. It doesn't take long to realize that there is no love, joy, or peace in dependency. Sooner or later the relationship is ruled by unending confusion, conflict, and crises.

In the book *How to Survive the Loss of Love,* poet Peter McWilliams captures the emotions like this:

> What do I do
> now that you're gone?
>
> Well, when there's
> nothing else going on,
> which is quite often,
> I sit in a corner and
> I cry
> until I am
> too numbed
> to feel.
>
> Paralyzed motionless
> for awhile, nothing

moving
inside or out.

Then I think
how much I miss you.
Then I feel
fear
pain
loneliness
desolation.

Then
I cry
until I am
too numbed
to feel.

Interesting pastime

the sun will rise
in a few minutes

it's been doing it
—regularly—
for as long as I
can remember.

Maybe I should
pin my hopes
on important,
but often unnoticed,
certainties
like that,

not on such relatively
trivial matters as
whether you will ever
love me or not.[1]

WHERE DO I START?

Once you have decided your relationships need to
change, where do you start? The following steps can help
you chart the course to emotional health.

RECOGNIZE HOW THE RELATIONSHIP STARTED

Dependencies always begin with good feelings. Dependency says:

1. I like how I feel when you notice and care about me.
2. I like how I feel when I take care of you and run interference for you.
3. I like how it feels to have my father's approval.
4. I like how I feel when my husband talks to me.
5. I like how I feel when my secretary asks, "Is there anything else you want?"
6. I like how I feel when my boss says, "You work circles around the rest of the typing pool."

In and of itself, there is nothing wrong with wanting to feel good. The problem arises when you become addicted to how a person makes you feel and are willing to do anything to see that feeling continue, even if the pain far outweighs the pleasure.

It's the addiction that distorts the relationship. In his book *The Freedom We Crave,* William Lenters describes the power of addiction.

> Addiction is an intensifying experience which grows out of someone's habitual response to something that has special meaning to him or her. That behavior produces feelings of safety, reassurance, affirmation, even pleasure. It is our nature to repeat that which produces pleasure, affirmation, reassurance, and safety. As the addictive process grows in intensity, providing the desired result, we gradually lose our power to choose for or against the activity. Instead, we impulsively, even compulsively, repeat the activity or return to the object of our affection. We don't have it anymore; it has us.[2]

Each of us feels the desire for belonging, for importance, for intimacy. God has given us a way to relate to one another and to him so that our need to "feel good" through relationship can be fully satisfied. Unfortunately, many of us have no idea how to relate to God or to our fellow human beings in any way other than "this makes me feel good." So we are very vulnerable to a relationship that offers to fulfill that need. But once we are into it, we realize something is very wrong. It's extremely painful to try to change the relationship or get out of it because we remember how good "feeling good" felt.

RECOGNIZE ADDICTIVE AND AUTHENTIC LOVE

Look at your relationships and try to distinguish addictive love (emotional dependence) from authentic love (emotional interdependence).

Addictive love says:

1. I can't live without you. You give my life meaning.
2. You make me feel valuable. When I'm with you, I am somebody.
3. I can't make it on my own.
4. I want you to be a total part of my life, and I want to be a total part of yours.
5. All of the hard times are worth the good times. I will be here forever, no matter what happens.
6. I can't bear to think of you sharing your thoughts and feelings with someone else. You are the only one who has ever understood me.
7. You should be sensitive to my needs. I have feelings, you know, and I need you to take that into consideration.
8. If you really care, you will treat me the way I need to be treated to feel good.

Authentic love says:

1. I can live without you, but I choose not to.

2. I'm a valuable person, and you affirm that value to me.

3. I can make it on my own. Having you as part of my life makes it easier.

4. We are two separate people with two individual lives to lead. I encourage you to pursue your interests, and I will pursue mine. This kind of space and diversity is good for us.

5. I believe love should seek another's highest good. To the best of my ability, I will do that for you, even if sometimes I fail.

6. We are richer for sharing our lives with other people. I encourage you to have other close relationships.

7. Mutuality is the glue that holds us together. I enjoy you, and in that enjoyment, I find that many of my needs for importance, belonging, and intimacy are met.

8. I will accept the way you show me you care about me. Sometimes I may have to ask you about your actions, but generally, I will take at face value what you say and do.

Having compared the two types of love, you may recognize that your understanding of love and relationships is very jaded. This can be a real shock. Yet sometimes it takes this shock to open our eyes to the danger of codependency. Occasionally the shock will be so great that you will become fearful of any kind of relationship—even healthy ones.

Proceed with caution. Don't panic or do anything rash. Beware of cutting yourself off from the people who can enrich your life and in whose lives you can be a treasure.

RECOGNIZE THE PROBLEMS
DEPENDENCY CREATES

1. *A loss of choices*. Once you are locked into a dependent relationship, obligation becomes ruler. To keep

things from changing, to keep the status quo, you find yourself doing things you never thought you would do and becoming what you never thought you would be.

Deception and half-truths become second nature as you try to cover any tracks that might cause conflict with the other person. It becomes a game you play against your better judgment as you are torn between the obligations of meeting the other person's needs and your belief that "no one should live this way."

2. *A loss of creative energy*. A codependent relationship saps your time and energy. Energy will seem to ooze out of you as you deal with the relationship. Constant crises and conflict pull on your thoughts even when you are not face-to-face with the other person. Sleep is often slow coming as you rehearse the details of the latest conflict and mentally search for answers that will improve the situation.

Guilt for not being able to make the relationship work can crush your confidence as you try to be creative. Your mind will often be a blur as you attempt to concentrate on the project at hand. You will find all of your creative energy being thrown into a remedy for your latest relationship crisis. Other interests grow dim.

3. *A loss of perspective on other people*. A codependent relationship is consuming. Therefore other people who are important to you will be put on hold while you give attention to keeping the relationship afloat. At the time, you may not see that you are slighting others. You pay attention to them, but a part of you is always distracted by the dependent relationship. You don't think it's noticeable. But after you have regained your perspective, you will see that sometimes those whom you love the most have suffered from your bondage. Spouses, parents, siblings, other friends, and children may see what is happening but say little or nothing because it's hard to convince someone

who is locked in a dependency that they really are dependent.

4. *A loss of personhood.* A codependent relationship will swallow you in a minute. Usually the weaker of the two people swallows the other by expressing needs, hanging on, manipulating, crying, begging, pleading, and accusing. The stronger of the two, feeling very responsible, will deny his or her own feelings and limit his or her behavior to make the weaker partner feel more secure.

5. *A loss of a dream.* Because codependent relationships start off with such a promising beginning, it's disappointing to realize that what you thought you had—a relationship on which you could depend for security, acceptance, approval, and value—was only a dream. The early intensity is overshadowed by conflict. The promises and hopes of "forever" are lost in the reality that "forever" is a very long time when you are caught in an addiction that never can be good for you or for the person you thought you loved.

6. *A loss of fellowship with the Lord.* A codependent relationship can dull your desire for fellowship with the Lord. People in codependent relationships often find they spend most of their prayer time talking to God about conflicts with the other person. They lose the delight of simply enjoying his presence.

Another reason for broken fellowship is that addiction to a person is sin. Remember, the Bible says, "You shall have no other gods before me" (Ex. 20:3). Anything or anyone who sits in the place that God should rightfully occupy in your life causes you to sin. That is just hard, cold reality, and when we sin, no matter what kind of circumstances we have come out of, we are responsible. It can be so hard to see something that started out so right and seemed "given by God" become sin. But part of the healing process is to come to the point of recognizing a dependent relationship as sin.

Lori Rentzel, the young woman who first introduced me to the whole idea of dependency, writes, "Whether or not physical involvement exists, sin enters the picture when a friendship becomes a dependent relationship. If we have been enjoined to seek first the kingdom of God, making the Lord Jesus Christ the center of our doing and being, then transgression has taken place when a relationship—any relationship—is made central to existence instead of God. God must be the provider of personal security because a human being ends up doing so only imperfectly."[3]

I would like to inject a note here about discipling relationships. Many believers have experienced the subtle infiltration of dependency into relationships in which the primary goal was discipleship. The very nature of this kind of one-on-one, teacher-student situation is fraught with the potential of dependency unless the discipler is very mature and aware of the hazards of dependency.

More than once, I've seen the joy in the eyes of an older Christian who has found a new convert to teach the ways of the Lord. In the proper context, the joy is genuine and legitimate. But it doesn't take much for the relationship to move beyond teaching the ways of the Lord.

Beware of the warning signs of codependency in discipling relationships. Social get-togethers become more and more significant. The emotionally dependent person schedules "just-the-two-of-us" activities. The disciple finds it hard to make decisions without consulting the discipler. And soon the entanglement is so intense that it would take the proverbial stick of dynamite to disengage it. And the sad thing is, it all started under the banner of learning the will and ways of Jesus Christ, the one who came to free us from ourselves and the bent, twisted, distorted thinking that makes us so vulnerable to dependencies.

THE ROAD TO HEALING

Recognition of the problem is the starting point for healing. Until the familiar feelings are identified as painful, unnecessary, and sinful, a cure can't be effected. Once you have recognized the problem, then look to the Lord for his healing power.

CONFESS

Confess your dependency as sin. To confess means to agree with God that it is sin to depend on the ongoing presence and support of another person to provide security, value, importance, and intimacy. Tell him that you have no desire to continue in sin, to continue putting someone else in his position. Remember that "If we confess our sins, he is faithful and just and will forgive us our sins and purify us from all unrighteousness" (1 John 1:9).

Thank him for forgiving and purifying you. Realize that because of his purification, you don't have to see yourself as a dependent person.

You are free from the bondage. Jesus said, "You will know the truth, and the truth will set you free" (John 8:32). You now know the truth and have been freed from the thinking that leads to dependency. Jesus is the binder of broken hearts and the only one who can promise, "I will never desert you, nor will I ever forsake you" (Heb. 13:5NASB). You know that only the Lord can "keep you from all harm" (Ps. 121:7). Only the Lord loves you "with an everlasting love" (Jer. 31:3).

Rehearse these truths over and over because the battle is not over yet. You are breaking an addiction that has captured your emotions.

REPENT

To repent means to have a change of mind with a change of direction. It is critical for you to see the relationship as sin, to see the losses that occur when you are entangled in it, and to recognize your own responsibility. It is even more critical to do something about it. You can't continue in the relationship. It's a no-win situation. That doesn't mean that you immediately bail out of a marriage, disown your parents, dump your friend, quit your job, or fire your employee. It does mean that you *stop the unhealthy way of relating*. The people live on as valuable, important people, but you must view the codependent relationship as dead. It is totally unacceptable for you to continue relating in the way you have in the past.

If the relationship is tainted by illicit sex, then you must run, not walk, away from the person and the environment in which you encounter him or her, even if it means quitting your job, firing an employee, or cutting all contact with a friend with whom you have been involved.

You must decide to take control of a situation that has been in control of you. When you have a change of mind, you will be able to execute a change of direction. To see the sickness and sadness of your addiction will give you the motivation you need to turn from it and pursue health.

The process of turning will be excruciatingly painful. In fact, you may feel as if you are having surgery without anesthesia. It will seem horribly invasive and cruel as you plunge the knife into this relationship that has been so much a part of your life. You will have difficulty hearing yourself say that it's over to a person who has consumed much of your attention, probably for years. But you must be able to say, "This relationship is over. It is dead. I love you, but I can no longer continue relating to you in the ways we have related. I have come to understand that the way we relate to one another is sin. I have looked to you (or you have looked to me) for security, importance, value, and intimacy. In a strange way, you (I) have become necessary for my (your) well-being. I assume responsibility for allowing this relationship to reach this state. Neither one of us is happy, and we don't enjoy peace. Someday we may be able to relate to one another as mature, Christian adults, but for right now, we must give one another time to heal, to learn, and to grow without interference in the process God is wanting to complete in our lives."

Don't be surprised if you are met with a flurry of tears and defensiveness. The other person in the relationship may not be ready to repent. But that's okay. In the long run, you both will benefit from your action. Be firm, be loving, be kind—and be on your way. Don't get sucked into hours of "I don't understand . . . please help me understand" conversations.

This way of closing a relationship is, of course, not applicable to parents or spouses. With them it's important to appeal to their sense of family, to express your love, and to ask that they respect your request to be freed from the dependence. Of course, it will not be that easy. In fact it may be impossible to discuss it. If you know beforehand that a talk is out of the question, just decide in your heart what you believe you should do and take it all to the Lord, asking him to work in their lives. Ask him for the strength and courage you need to be the wife, mother, husband, father, child that you need to be.

OBEY

Obedience is where the going gets tough. Following through on your repentance will take the total grace of God in your life. This type of situation rarely goes smoothly because your emotions have been rubbed raw over a long period of time. But each step of obedience will bring you closer to healing.

1. *Get involved with other people.* More than one is preferable. The last thing you want to do is to fall into another dependent relationship. Don't fool yourself by thinking it can't happen to you again.

The first weeks after breaking a dependent relationship will be one of your most vulnerable times. The time you used to spend together will be dead on your hands unless you plan for what you will do. It will be incredibly tempting to pick up the phone and start the cycle again unless you are prepared to handle the pain of loneliness and boredom.

2. *Determine that your pain will not be wasted.* Spend time with the Lord, asking him to teach you what you need to know about your root problem. The hurts will never be healed unless you are willing to let the Lord teach you and touch you in your heart's deep places that you have always protected with the excuse, "Well, that's just the way I am." If you fail to let the Lord minister to you during this time, you'll find yourself in the same predicament again.

3. *Let go of it.* Because this relationship has been a part of you for so long, you will miss the other person and long for the good times and the feeling of security you once had. You may end up torturing yourself with a lot of "what if's" and "if only's" if you don't let it go by yielding it up to God.

SURRENDER

In counseling, a technique is used called "emotional detachment." It means to let go. Believers can take it a step beyond and let go by giving it up to God. We call that releasing it, committing it to God, or surrender.

Emotional detachment holds within it the concept that you don't have to carry the weight of the emotion anymore. You choose to stop feeling hurt, anger or resentment. You reach a point of understanding that to continue your feelings could lead to your own emotional/physical ruin. To continue to be codependent can bring on bitterness or even hatred. Often it brings on physical symptoms and even allows disease to attack a body wracked with emotional stress.

Once you realize that the Lord cares more than you do, you can let go of your painful emotions and walk in obedience to what you know is his will. It's *his* responsibility to comfort the other person in the relationship. It's *his* responsibility to strengthen and comfort you in whatever way you need to be comforted. It's *his* job to take care of your dependent parents—give them to him. It's *his* problem to change your mate. Quit bearing that burden and give it to him. "Cast all your anxiety on him because he cares for you" (1 Peter 5:7).

It may seem coldhearted to talk about emotional detachment and surrender, but consider the alternatives. You have a Burden Bearer who is willing to carry your burden for you, to release you from those emotions that torment you. So isn't it logical that you can trust him to take care of the whole situation?

> In the end we must be prepared simply to surrender who we are to God. That's neither a pious cliché nor a shrug of the shoulders that leaves our flesh up for grabs. Rather, it is a very intentional, painful, spiritual discipline in which we lay who we are at God's feet, in effect saying, "Lord, here I am. This is how I am. Take me, take all of me. I can't handle it myself."[4]

My friend, there are no pat answers. There are no formulas or systems that can be applied to make the healing of these sad, painful situations easy. In fact, there is no formula that works 100 percent of the time for everyone. These relationships are part of the suffering and struggle we face between birth and death. They are part of the promised trials and testing that allow us to see if the faith we claim is genuine. And as painful as it is to wake up and realize just what kind of situation you are in, you can be sure our God is watching with his father-heart-eyes, longing, straining, squinting to see his children make it through in victory.

As his children, we may skip right past the bars, the

pubs, the street dealers, and the crack houses. We may never come home drunk, beat our children, kill someone, or wind up living on a downtown street because we have lost everything to drugs. But as we gather our skirts around us and clutch our Bibles to our breasts, may we see ourselves as people who are just as needy. May we see what we have done as we have looked to one another for the value, the intimacy, and the security that only God, our Father, can give.

• • •

You can be made whole. You can be free of your emotional dependency. You will get better. It will take time.

—— JS ——

9

Maintaining Healthy Relationships

Codependency is like the gorgeous green kudzu vine that grows along the roadsides in the southern United States. Visitors driving through the area often comment on its beauty as they see it for the first time. But for the natives of the region, who have seen this wild, untamable vine choke the life out of acres of healthy forest, there is no beauty at all. There is nothing good about kudzu, just as there is nothing good about codependency. To the untrained and unsuspecting person, it may look perfectly harmless or even desirable. For the person who has lived with it and survived, there is a healthy fear of ever letting it take root again.

SAFEGUARDS AGAINST EMOTIONAL DEPENDENCY

Several safeguards can keep you from future dependent relationships. These will require discipline because you will be learning new relating skills, which may seem uncomfortable at first. These will also require a keen memory. If you forget how dark the dungeon of dependency is, you can easily be tempted to return to another codependent relationship. Since dependent relationships always feel good at first, you must keep up your guard or your temptation to "feel good" will outweigh your determination to "be good."

DEVELOP A HEALTHY SELF-CONCEPT

A healthy self-concept is your first line of defense against any future entanglement. This idea may frighten many believers. I understand. The thought that some humanistic philosophy may influence me to value myself too highly frightens me too. However, if I am to have a truly healthy self-concept, I will want to know and understand God's perspective of who I am. I will want nothing more—and nothing less. It is just as sinful to devalue what God thinks of me as it is to think more highly of myself than he does.

You may wonder how low self-esteem makes you a target for emotional dependency. If you don't have a healthy concept of God, yourself, and others, then you'll be very skeptical. When God says he sees every bird that falls, you'll think, "Maybe he knows about the birds, but I doubt he even knows my name." You will think of yourself as inadequate apart from your attachment to another person. Although God has said you are complete in him (Col. 2:10), you still feel incomplete without someone to stand beside you to make up for your shortcomings. Your feelings about other people will be similar to the feelings you have about God. Although you love them and want to be important to them, you really doubt if they care about you even though they may constantly assure and reassure you. If you can't receive God's love and the love of others, the problem is yours. Your perception of your own value keeps you from accepting the evaluation of God and others, and that ultimately affects the way you feel about yourself. You will sincerely doubt that they find any value in you.

CHOOSE TO VALUE GOD

God's Word has a cleansing, renewing power. Since our minds are the source of all behavior, we must learn to change our minds to bring change in our behavior.

God gives a great deal of instruction in Scripture about how we are to think. But he tells us only one way that our thinking can be changed for good. In Romans 12:2, he says, "Do not be conformed to this world, but be transformed by the renewing of your mind." Our minds can be changed only as we allow God's thoughts to cleanse our thoughts, which don't naturally line up with his. In fact, God says, "My thoughts are not your thoughts and my ways are not your ways" (Isa. 55:8).

Very often our thoughts about God's nature are distorted, bent, and twisted. People who come from homes in which the father was not a healthy role model often find it hard to see clearly who their heavenly Father is. We need to renew our minds by looking afresh at what the Scripture says about God. Appendix C lists some of God's attributes—his characteristics. Read over that list and consciously try to renew your awareness of who he is. You may even want to memorize some of these verses.

Another effective exercise for renewing your mind is personalizing Scripture. Put verses throughout your home about the great value God has placed in you and the unconditional love he has for you. Use the following verses as a pattern for personalizing verses that are meaningful to you (You may want to personalize the verses found in Appendix B, Your Value in Christ).

> I know the plans I have for you, Jan, plans to prosper you and not to harm you, plans to give you hope and a future (Jer. 29:11).

> Jan, I love you with an everlasting love; therefore I have drawn you with loving-kindness (Jer. 31:3).

> Jan, do not fear, for I am with you; do not be dismayed, for I am your God. I will strengthen you and help you; I will uphold you with my righteous right hand (Isa. 41:10).

> Jan, you are precious in my sight, you are honored and I love you (Isa. 43:4 NASB).

Another helpful resource for renewing your mind is a good devotional book. Find authors whose thoughts are biblically accurate and meaningful—authors whose souls connect to your soul. Amy Carmichael, Marie Chapian, and Max Lucado have been those kinds of authors for me.

You may wonder why I have recommended that you saturate yourself in the Word of God and in reading how other Christians have been able to communicate the relevancy of their walk with him. It's because your self-concept is in your mind, and anything you can do to cleanse your mind and build new perceptions is important to your healing. Your relationship to God is absolutely essential to finding the wholeness for which you longed and the security for which you searched when you settled for dependent relationships.

When you have a correct perspective of God, then you will be able to have a correct perspective of the other people and events in your life. Your healing hinges on knowing God as he really is, not as you have perceived him to be, based on the actions of parents and authority figures who were affected by the same bent, twisted, distorted thinking you have experienced. I can't stress that enough. *Until you have pursued knowing God as he is, you will not find healing from codependency*. He promises, "If you seek for me you will find me" (Jer. 29:13). Even if you have been a Christian for many years, we still live in a fallen world and our perceptions of God can be distorted by the people around us. It's your responsibility and mine to discover an accurate picture of God—to know him as he is.

CHOOSE TO VALUE YOURSELF

People will value you according to the value you place on yourself. It seems like ancient history now, but not long ago mothers told daughters that girls who allowed boys to touch them in private places were "cheap." What the mothers were trying to say was, "You are worth more than that. You have value apart from the momentary attention a boy will give you so he can explore your body. A girl who thinks no more of herself than to let that happen has a cheap sense of her own value. And as your mother, I'm telling you, you are wonderfully valuable!"

The same thing is true in the way we allow people to treat us and the way we treat others. If you value yourself as a creation of God, then it's not acceptable to be treated as an object, an animal, or a slave. You may be the victim of someone's abuse once. The other person may be stronger and more powerful physically or emotionally, but if you truly value yourself, you will not be a victim twice. You are of greater value than to allow someone to abuse and use you for personal gratification.

Please understand. I'm not talking about an attitude that is touchy and ready to take on all comers at the drop of a hat just because someone disagrees or gives you a hard time. That's not godly. Jesus says we are to be long-suffering, patient, loving, forgiving, and tenderhearted. I'm talking instead about people who feel incapable of making a choice because they feel so unworthy. They remain in circumstances in which they feel their only way of being heard is to scream, cry, beg, or plead. They hang on to relationships that are unhealthy because they are afraid to say, "No more. I love you, but I can no longer relate in this way." They are impotent and miserable.

Sue is a perfect example. She is married to a man who is arrogant and difficult. He has convinced Sue that she is small-minded and dull, although she is very industrious, well educated, and personable.

Their teenage children are arrogant and difficult as well. They mock their mother and belittle her with their father's full support and, at times, his participation.

Sue vacillates between feeling very guilty for being unable to please her family and feeling angry that they will not respond to her many attempts to win them by her kindness.

Her husband's contempt has increased with the years until now he wants her out of the house.

Sue is a believer who desperately wants to honor her

marriage vows and for twenty-five years has bent to her husband's every demand. Now she is left as a "throwaway." I'm convinced Sue is in this situation because she has missed this one fact: She is valuable. She isn't cheap. But she has allowed her husband to think of her and to treat her as cheap.

Now Sue sees herself as disposable, causing her to act in a way that confirms her husband's feelings about her. If she had viewed herself as valuable, her marriage would still be a difficult one, but she would not have spent the last twenty-five years trying to make herself acceptable to a man who finds her contemptible. I'm not saying that the marriage would have been over. Divorce is not the only way to cope. I'm saying that people who value themselves and others are not willing to allow a relationship to be chaotic day in and day out, one day scurrying around to please and the next day begging to be loved.

To devalue yourself is to devalue others. By allowing her husband to demean her, Sue has cheapened both of them. Of course, it is easy for me to say "If only she had . . . ," but the principle is important if she is to break out of this mentality.

If love is seeking another person's highest good, then to allow people you love to belittle and berate you consistently is to allow them to act inconsistently with the highest good for themselves. We must learn to confront lovingly, to deal with our anger, and to work toward positive change. This requires work and discipline. When confronted with someone's demeaning behavior, most of us want to retaliate and take our own vengeance. That's not God's way. And it never accomplishes permanent change.

CHOOSE TO VALUE OTHERS

God says our relationships are so important to him that we "must no longer live as the Gentiles do, in the futility of their thinking. They are darkened in their understanding" (Eph. 4:17–18).

As Christians we don't have to act and interact like everyone else. We are people of value—people who have the high privilege of acting as if we have been bought with a price. God gives us an example of how people of value treat one another: "Therefore, laying aside falsehood, speak truth, each one of you, with his neighbor, for we are members of one another. Be angry, and yet do not sin; do not let the sun go down on your anger, and do not give the devil an opportunity" (Eph. 4:25–27 NASB).

As Christians, we are to be honest with one another, not holding back from speaking the truth in love because we are afraid to lose approval or our imagined security. We are to handle our anger in a way that will avoid the long-term damage of bitterness, which, according to Hebrews 12:15, will defile many if we let it take root. Anger is to be dealt with when it occurs and then let go. Unfortunately, if we don't value ourselves, then we probably won't feel worthy to express anger, no matter how right that anger is. The Bible says, "go ahead and be angry, get it out in the open in a way that will not affect everyone around and then let it go before you go to bed. Don't keep rehearsing it in your mind, because holding on to your anger will never accomplish God's righteousness in your life or in anyone else's" (James 1:19–20), paraphrased.

As people who are valued and loved, we can deal with the truth about ourselves and others. As Christians, our goal should be to conform to the behavior outlined in Ephesians 4: 31–31: "Get rid of all bitterness, rage and anger, brawling and slander, along with every form of malice. Be kind and compassionate to one another, forgiving each other, just as in Christ God also forgave you."

We have an opportunity to put away our old lifestyle with all of its perverted, twisted ways of relating. Because we are valuable, we don't have to prove anything to anyone to make us more valuable. We can relax, give others the benefit of the doubt, and forgive whoever has wronged us.

I don't want to belabor the point, dear friend, but there is a difference between giving the benefit of the doubt, forgiving, and becoming a scapegoat for another's twisted thinking. Sometimes it's totally appropriate to remove yourself from a situation. When you do this, you are not being unforgiving or unkind; you are being wise. If you have tried talking, if you have sought counseling, if you have prayed fervently and the situation is still demeaning to the value you both have, then you need to consider removing yourself from the relationship, whether it is with your parents, your spouse, your friend, or your employer.

Your goal should always be reconciliation because that's God's goal. However, reconciliation isn't always possible. Sometimes people refuse to change. But you can't be responsible for how another person reacts. You are responsible only for your own actions. You are responsible to live this precious life God has given you to the very fullest. To continue to believe the lie that you and others are of little or no value is to deny the Lord Jesus. You were worth his blood. You were worth his agony. Therefore, it's your responsibility to act like the valuable, loved person you really are and to treat others as valuable and loved. To look to another person to find value, esteem, and security not only cheapens the relationship you have with the Lord Jesus Christ but it also puts more responsibility on another's shoulders than that person should have to bear.

My friend, the choice is yours. You can continue to cling to a relationship that will eventually destroy you. To be honest, that will seem like the easiest thing to do when you begin to see the changes that are necessary. Change is never easy. It requires strong motivation and discipline.

CHOOSE TO VALUE DISCIPLINE

If you have been in pain as you have read this book, then you have the motivation. If you see yourself and those you love in these pages and if you ache deep down inside for the hurt and discouragement that never seem to go away, then you have the motivation.

Now the question is, Will you withstand the discipline? Will you pay the price of retraining your thoughts?

The Scriptures remind us, "No discipline seems pleasant at the time, but painful. *Later on,* however, it produces a harvest of righteousness and peace" (Heb. 12:11, emphasis added). The Scriptures also say God has given us everything we need to live godly lives (2 Peter 1:3). He has told us that if we are Christians, we have all we need to endure the discipline that will bring us to wholeness.

The discipline will be for your good, not to make you a loner who is afraid of loving, but to make you a lover who can love more deeply than you've ever loved before. Healthy love is the greatest capacity you have. As you learn to love God as he is, yourself as you are, and others as they are, you will someday reach the goal of your discipline—a righteousness that manifests itself in pure, unselfish, transforming love. You will learn to lay down your expectations before they discourage you. You will learn to offer up your disappointments before they depress you. You will learn to stare down your fear of rejection with the steady gaze of one who is confident in who he or she is.

Relationships will never bring you total joy and peace. But you will be able to meet the challenges of relationships with the maturity of one who has lived through a war—and won.

•   •   •

My friend, codependency will strangle the life out of the most precious relationships you have. It will warp your trust of God, twist your feelings for your parents, pervert your love for your mate, distort your care for your children, and drive away your friends. To remain codependent is to live as a captive in a life designed to be free.

You are loved and you are valuable! You are worthy to give and receive love. Today is your opportunity to show the world how loved people relate to God, themselves, and others!

My prayer for you is that you will accept the challenge to take the first step toward wholeness in your relationships, to dare to believe God, and to depend on Jesus Christ to be your companion for life.

—— JS ——

Appendix A

How Can I Have a Relationship to Christ?

1. **What does it mean to have a relationship to Christ?** To have a relationship to Christ, you must be saved—you must be born again.

   Being saved refers to salvation from the penalty of sin by entering into a personal relationship to Jesus Christ. It means that you can live victoriously during this lifetime and go to heaven when you die.

   Being born again refers to a spiritual rebirth that takes place when you acknowledge sin in your life, repent (agree with God about sin), accept Jesus Christ's payment for sin, and commit your life to him. To be born again is to be saved, to have salvation, to be a Christian.

2. **What is sin?**

   - Failure to meet God's standards
   - Doing your own thing
   - Having your own way
   - Disobeying God in thought, word, or deed

   All we like sheep have gone astray, we have turned every one to his own way . . ." (Isaiah 53:6).

   So any person who knows what is right to do but does not do it, to him it is a sin (James 4:17).
   (Verses from THE AMPLIFIED BIBLE).

3. **Who are sinners? Aren't most people basically good?** Every person has sinned.

   All have sinned and are falling short of the honor and glory which God bestows and receives (Rom. 3:23 AMPLIFIED).

Therefore as sin came into the world through one man and death as the result of sin, so death spread to all men [no one being able to stop it or to escape its power] because all men sinned (Rom. 5:12 AMPLIFIED).

For the wages which sin pays is death; but the [bountiful] free gift of God is eternal life through [in union with] Jesus Christ, our Lord (Rom. 6:23 AMPLIFIED).

4. **Why is sin so bad?** Sin separates you from God.

But your iniquities have separated you from your God; your sins have hidden his face from you, so that he will not hear (Isa. 59:2).

[God's] eyes are too pure to look on evil; you [God] cannot tolerate wrong (Hab. 1:13).

5. **Since sin has separated me from God, is there any hope?** Yes. God has done everything necessary to provide a way for your salvation.

The Lord is not slow in keeping his promise, as some understand slowness. He is patient with you, not wanting anyone to perish, but everyone to come to repentance (2 Peter 3:9).

For God so greatly loved and dearly prized the world that He [even] gave up His only-begotten (unique) Son, so that whosoever believes in (trusts, clings to, relies on) Him shall not perish—come to destruction, be lost—but have eternal (everlasting) life (John 3:16 AMPLIFIED).

But to as many as did receive and welcome Him, He gave the authority [power, privilege, right] to become the children of God, that is, to those who believe in—adhere to, trust in, rely on—His name (John 1:12 AMPLIFIED).

This is how God showed his love among us: He sent his one and only Son into the world that we might live through him. This is love: not that we loved God, but that he loved us and sent his Son as an atoning sacrifice for our sins (1 John 4:9–10).

6. **How did Jesus provide salvation?** His death on the cross paid for sin. He accepted the penalty for your sin and paid the price.

> But he was pierced for our transgressions, he was crushed for our iniquities; the punishment that brought us peace was upon him, and by his wounds we are healed. We all, like sheep, have gone astray, each of us has turned to his own way; and the Lord has laid on him the iniquity of us all (Isa. 53:5–6).

> For our sake He made Christ [virtually] to be sin Who knew no sin, so that in and through Him we might become [endued with, viewed as in and examples of] the righteousness of God—what we ought to be, approved and acceptable and in right relationship to Him, by His goodness (2 Cor. 5:21 AMPLIFIED).

7. **How can I be saved?** You can be saved by entering into a personal relationship to Jesus Christ through trusting in (believing in, having faith in) him and his payment for sin. You must believe that . . .

> Christ died for our sins according to the Scriptures, that he was buried, that he was raised on the third day according to the Scriptures (1 Cor. 15:3b–4).

8. **What will happen when I do this?**
   a. Your sins will be forgiven. And because your sins are forgiven, they will no longer separate you from God.

> In Him we have redemption (deliverance and salvation) through His blood, the remission (forgiveness) of our offenses (shortcomings and trespasses), in accordance with the riches and the generosity of His gracious favor (Eph. 1:7 AMPLIFIED).

b. You will be sealed with the Holy Spirit of God.

And you also were included in Christ when you heard the word of truth, the gospel of your salvation. Having believed, you were marked in him with a seal, the promised Holy Spirit (Eph. 1:13).

c. You will have eternal life.

He who has the Son has life; he who does not have the Son of God does not have life (1 John 5:12).

9. **I do want to be saved. How do I do it?** Talk to God. Tell him how you feel. You might say something like this:

God, I know that I have sinned—in thought, word, and deed. I have lived for myself and not for you. Thank you for sending Jesus to pay for my sin by giving his life on the cross. I want Jesus to come into my heart and be my Savior.
Amen.

10. **Must I do anything else?** Tell others about your decision to be a Christian.

Because if you acknowledge and confess with your lips that Jesus is Lord and in your heart believe (adhere to, trust in and rely on the truth) that God raised Him from the dead, you will be saved. For with the heart a person believes (adheres to, trusts in and relies on Christ) and so is justified (declared righteous, acceptable to God), and with the mouth he confesses—declares openly and speaks out freely his faith—and confirms [his] salvation (Rom. 10:9–10 AMPLIFIED).

Now that you are a Christian, you are a part of the family of God (John 1:12) and you can never lose that position. You have been reborn.

Therefore if any person is (ingrafted) in Christ, the Messiah, he is (a new creature altogether,) a new creation; the old (previous moral and spiritual

condition) has passed away. Behold, the fresh and
new has come! (2 Cor. 5:17 AMPLIFIED).

How does being a Christian, being born again,
change a person who is codependent? Jesus Christ is now
in his rightful position in your life. He has become your
master, owner, friend, and companion for life. The Holy
Spirit lives within you and gives you power to live in
obedience to God. You now have the power not to sin.
Since he still gives you a free will, the choice is under your
control. He simply enables you to make a choice.

> We know that our old (unrenewed) self was nailed
> to the cross with Him in order that (our) body,
> [which is the instrument] of sin, might be made
> ineffective and inactive for evil, that we might no
> longer be the slaves of sin (Rom. 6:6 AMPLIFIED).

> Let not sin therefore rule as king in your mortal
> (short-lived, perishable) bodies, to make you yield
> to their cravings and be subject to their lusts and
> evil passions. Do not continue offering or yielding
> your bodily members [and faculties] to sin as
> instruments (tools) of wickedness. But offer and
> yield yourselves to God as though you have been
> raised from the dead to [perpetual] life, and your
> bodily members [and faculties] to God, presenting
> them as implements of righteousness. For sin shall
> not [any longer] exert dominion over you, since
> now you are not under Law [as slaves], but under
> grace—as subjects of God's favor and mercy
> (Rom. 6:12–14 AMPLIFIED).

As you prayerfully read and meditate upon Scripture, saturating your mind with God's Word, he will
transform your life (Rom. 12:2).

As you begin to know him as the faithful, loyal,
trustworthy, loving Savior, you will realize he is the only
one who can truthfully say, "I will never leave you nor
forsake you." He alone is worthy of your total depen-

dence. His greatest desire is to have a relationship with you, to love you, and to have you take him at his word.

Appendix B

Your Value in Christ

These Scripture verses will help you to renew your mind. Read each verse, asking God to show you what he thinks of you.

You are a new creation (2 Cor. 5:17).

You are a child of God. You belong to him (John 1:12; 1 Peter 2:9).

You are a gift from God to Jesus (John 17:9, 12, 24).

You are greatly loved (Rom. 8:35–39).

You have been drawn by God (John 6:44).

You have been called by God (Rom. 8:28, 30)

You have been chosen by God (Eph. 1:4).

You are in Jesus' prayers (John 17:9; Heb. 7:25).

You are his friend (John 15:14–15).

You have access to God through Jesus (Eph. 2:18; 3:12).

You are being conformed to his image (Rom. 8:29).

You have been sanctified and justified with God (1 Cor. 6:11).

You are a co-heir with Christ (Rom. 8:17).

You are forgiven for all your sin (Col. 2:13).

You are not condemned (Rom. 8:1).

You have power over all sin (Rom. 6).

You can live victoriously through him (2 Cor. 2:14; Jude 24).

You are strengthened by him (Phil. 4:13).

You are God's workmanship (handiwork) (Eph. 2:10; Phil. 1:6; 2:13)

Your body is the temple of the Holy Spirit (1 Cor. 6:19).

You have God's Spirit within you (John 14:16; 2 Tim. 1:14).

You have all you need for life and godliness (2 Peter 1:3).

You have eternal life (John 3:16).

—— JS ——

Appendix C

The Attributes of God

What is God like? Can you really depend upon him to meet your deepest needs? Can he satisfy the longings of your heart?

To know the attributes of God—his characteristics—is to know he is trustworthy. As you get to know him, you will be able to relax with him, rely on him, and deepen your relationship until your longing to be loved, valued, and secure is satisfied in him.

God has chosen to reveal himself through his Word. As you look for him in Scripture, you will find him to be

Compassionate—God's compassion, his mercy, is demonstrated by his loving-kindness toward us. "The Lord is compassionate and gracious, slow to anger, abounding in love" (Ps. 103:8).

Faithful—God is loyal, devoted and worthy of our confidence. He can't lie. "Let us hold unswervingly to the hope we profess, for he who promised is faithful" (Heb. 10:23).

Holy—God is absolutely excellent in morality. "For the Mighty One has done great things for me—holy is his name" (Luke 1:49).

Immutable—God doesn't change. "Jesus Christ is the same yesterday and today and forever" (Heb. 13:8).

Infinite—God has no bounds or limits. "Oh, the depth of the riches of the wisdom and knowledge of God! How unsearchable his judgments, and his paths beyond tracing out!'' (Rom. 11:33).

Just—God always acts fairly and in accordance with his nature. "He is the Rock, his works are perfect, and all his ways are just. A faithful God who does no wrong, upright and just is he" (Deut. 32:4).

Long-suffering—God is patient, a characteristic that is associated with hope and mercy. "But you, O Lord, are a compassionate and gracious God, slow to anger, abounding in love and faithfulness" (Ps. 86:15).

Loving—God expresses his love in his actions toward us. His love is unconditional, sacrificial, and everlasting. It exists because of who he is and not because of anything deserved by those who receive it. "For I am convinced that neither death nor life, neither angels nor demons, neither the present nor the future, nor any powers, neither height nor depth, nor anything else in all creation, will be able to separate us from the love of God that is in Christ Jesus our Lord" (Rom. 8:38–39).

Omnipotent—God is almighty, all powerful—unlimited in power, authority, or ability. "Ah, sovereign Lord, you have made the heavens and the earth by your great power and outstretched arm. Nothing is too hard for you" (Jer. 32:17).

Omnipresent—God is present everywhere at the same time; he is never absent. "'Am I a God nearby,' declares the Lord, 'and not a God far away? Can anyone hide in secret places so that I cannot see him?' declares the Lord. 'Do not I fill heaven and earth?' declares the Lord" (Jer. 23:23–24).

Omniscient—God knows everything; he has infinite wisdom. "You know when I sit and when I rise; you perceive my thoughts from afar. You discern my going out and my lying down; you are familiar with all my ways. Before a

word is on my tongue you know it completely, O Lord"
(Ps. 139:2–4).

Righteous—God always does right and is free from any
wrong doing. "The Lord is righteous in all his ways and
loving toward all he has made" (Ps. 145:17).

Sovereign—God rules over all. He is supreme in his
position and is limited by no one. "Yours, O Lord, is the
greatness and the power and the glory and the majesty and
the splendor, for everything in heaven and earth is yours.
Yours, O Lord, is the kingdom; you are exalted as head
over all. Wealth and honor come from you; you are the
ruler of all things. In your hands are strength and power to
exalt and give strength to all. Now, our God, we give you
thanks, and praise your glorious name" (1 Chron. 29:11–
13). "The Lord reigns, he is robed in majesty; the Lord is
robed in majesty and is armed with strength. The world is
firmly established; it cannot be moved. Your throne was
established long ago; you are from all eternity" (Ps. 93:1–
2). "He does as he pleases with the powers of heaven and
the peoples of the earth. No one can hold back his hand or
say to him: 'What have you done?'" (Dan. 4:35b).

Truthful—God can't lie. "For the faith of God's elect and
the knowledge of the truth that leads to godliness—a faith
and knowledge resting on the hope of eternal life, which
God, who does not lie, promised before the beginning of
time" (Titus 1:1b–2).

Wrathful—God punishes sin. "Do not take revenge, my
friends, but leave room for God's wrath, for it is written:
'It is mine to avenge; I will repay,' says the Lord" (Rom.
12:19).

—— JS ——

Notes

Definition of Terms

[1]Ann Corwin, "When Work Makes You Sick," *Creative Loafing,* 1989.

[2]Melody Beattie, *Codependent No More* (New York: Harper & Row, 1987), 31.

Chapter 1—What's Wrong with Me?

1. Howard M. Halpern, *How to Break Your Addiction to a Person* (New York: Bantam, 1983), 99.
2. Ibid.
3. M. Scott Peck, *The Road Less Traveled,* (New York: Simon and Schuster, 1978), 100.
4. Ibid.

Chapter 3—Why Do I Act This Way?

1. David Seamands, *Healing for Damaged Emotions* (Wheaton, Ill.: Victor Books, 1981), 71–72.
2. R. Laird Harris, Gleason J. Archer, Jr., and Bruce K. Waltke, eds., *Theological Word Book of the Old Testament* (Chicago: Moody Press, 1980), 4–20.
3. Seamands, *Healing for Damaged Emotions,* 70.

Chapter 4—Codependency in Parent-Child Relationships

1. Claudia Black, *It Will Never Happen to Me!* (New York, NY: Ballantine Books, 1981), 77.
2. Gary Smalley and John Trent, *The Blessing* (Nashville: Nelson, 1986), 21.

Chapter 5—Codependency in Marriage

1. Ed Wheat, *Love Life for Every Married Couple* (Grand Rapids: Zondervan, 1980), 119–121.

2. Janet Geringer Woititz, *Adult Children of Alcoholics* (Pompano Beach, FL: Health Communications, 1983).
3. Ibid.
4. Janet G. Woititz, *Struggle for Intimacy* (Pompano Beach, FL: Health Communications, 1985), 31–33.
5. Marie Chapian, *Growing Closer* (Old Tappan, N.J.: Revell, 1986), 59.
6. Kay Marshall Strom, *In the Name of Submission* (Portland, Ore.: Multnomah Press, 1986), 52–53.
7. Ibid.
8. Wheat, *Love Life for Every Married Couple,* 120–121.

Chapter 6—Codependency in Friendship

1. Letty Cottin Pogrebin, *Among Friends* (New York: McGraw-Hill, 1987), 81.
2. R. J. Sternberg, "Measuring Love" (paper written for Yale University) as quoted in Pogrebin, *Among Friends,* 62–63.
3. Pogrebin, *Among Friends,* 80–81.
4. Gary Inrig, *Quality Friendship* (Chicago: Moody Press, 1981), 55.
5. Lori Thorkelson Rentzel, "Emotional Dependency," (San Raphael, Calif.: Exodus International, 1984), 1–2.
6. Charles M. Swindoll, *Come Before Winter* (Portland, Ore.: Multnomah Press, 1985), 186.
7. Pamela Reeve, "Relationships" (Portland, Ore.: Multnomah Press, 1982), 15.
8. Ibid., 16.

Chapter 7—What's Wrong with This Job?

1. Lois Mowday, *The Snare* (Colorado Springs: Navpress, 1988), 179–180.
2. Ibid.
3. "Homosexual Struggle," (Downers Grove, Ill.: Inter-Varsity Press, 1978).

Chapter 8—Help! I'm Dependent!

1. Melba Colgore, *How to Survive the Loss of Love* (New York: Bantam, 1976), 13–14.

2. William Lenters, *The Freedom We Crave* (Grand Rapids: Eerdmans, 1985), 38.
3. Rentzel, "Emotional Dependency."
4. Lenters, *The Freedom We Crave,* 47.